THE ACCUSING GHOST
OR
JUSTICE FOR CASEMENT

Roger Casement in 1914

THE ACCUSING GHOST
OR
JUSTICE FOR CASEMENT

by

ALFRED NOYES

LONDON
VICTOR GOLLANCZ LTD
1957

Printed in Great Britain by
The Camelot Press Ltd., London and Southampton

"There is a very strong opinion abroad—*The Times* gives expression to it this morning—that someone in authority 'inspired' a campaign of malignant and studied calumny against the prisoner which was not only not necessary to the course of justice, but calculated to pervert it."

> Letter from Professor J. H. Morgan, Reader in Constitutional Law to the Inns of Court, later Legal Adviser to American War Crimes Commission at Nuremberg, etc., written on the morning after the execution of Sir Roger Casement, to the Home Secretary.

To whom I answered: It is not the custom of the Romans to condemn any man before that he who is accused have his accusers present and have liberty to make his answer, to clear himself of the things laid to his charge.

Acts of the Apostles XXV, 15

FOREWORD

Before writing this book I carefully studied all the preceding biographies of Sir Roger Casement, his available letters and writings, including the Reports and statements which he sent in to the Foreign Office and which were published by His Majesty's Stationery Office; the *Diaries of Sir Roger Casement, His Mission to Germany and the Findlay Affair* (Arche Publishing Company, Munich); the various and varying narratives given by the head of the C.I.D., Sir Basil Thomson; *The Eyes of the Navy*, by Admiral Sir William James; *Famous Trials*, by Lord Birkenhead; the verbatim report of the State trial, as revised by that same shrewd lawyer; the *Life of Lord Carson*, by Marjoribanks and Colvin; and many biographies and memoirs of the time.

I am indebted to Senator Roger McHugh, representative of the National University of Ireland, for valuable new material, as well as for help from the National Library of Ireland; to Mr. Seamas MacCall, a relative of Sir Roger Casement, for valuable information and some photostatic copies of correspondence of Mrs. Sidney Parry (Gertrude Bannister); to Dr. Mackey, F.R.C.S., and to the Unionist Member for Belfast, Lieut.-Col. Montgomery Hyde, for valuable information; and to Mrs. Sowerby (Olivia Meynell) for letters to her father from Wilfrid Scawen Blunt.

The latest biography by Mr. René MacColl gives a vivid objective picture of various aspects of the case, but I fear he has been seriously misled (as I and many others were misled in 1916) by *copies* of the alleged diary which were shown to him between 1954 and 1956. In spite of his belief in the diary, however, he presses for authentication, which, if his evidence were satisfactory, would be unnecessary, and he quite rightly condemns the evasions of the Departments concerned.

I am particularly grateful to Mr. Michael Francis Doyle, Casement's American counsel, for several helpful letters in which he emphatically confirms my conclusions that the 'diaries' were fraudulent.

Innumerable side-lights upon the character of Sir Roger Casement are to be found in works not directly connected with him, as, to mention only a few, in the *Life and Letters of Joseph Conrad*; the *Diaries of Wilfrid Scawen Blunt*; the *Recollections of a Literary Man*, by Stephen Gwynn; and *Last Changes, Last Chances*, by H. W. Nevinson. I could not find one that did not testify to the fineness of Casement's moral character and to the truth of what in 1911 *The Times* said in an editorial: "Sir Roger Casement has deserved well of his countrymen and of mankind."

In view of the surreptitious campaign against that character, calculated, as Professor J. H. Morgan said, "to pervert the course of justice", the circumstances imperatively need examination.

The purpose of this book is not primarily biographical but a "cross-examination" in which the biographical facts are introduced as they bear upon the case and in which questions may sometimes be repeated from different angles in order to establish a truth.

"Truth," said the representative of the Home Office, "may be found to be many-sided." Let us, then, look at some of its hitherto hidden sides.

CHAPTER I

The ghost of Roger Casement is beating on the door.
W. B. YEATS.

SIR ROGER CASEMENT, an Irish Nationalist, was hanged at Pentonville Prison on August 3rd, 1916, for high treason. Under English law there was no doubt that he had incurred this charge—but in what circumstances?

The conduct of the prosecution was in many respects discreditable to the great tradition of English justice. Too late, and after the execution, this was emphasized by editorials in *The Times* and the *Manchester Guardian*. Even in the heat of war petitions for a reprieve were begun. The signatories included men of unquestioned loyalty and great distinction in many walks of life, science, art, literature and religion. Among them were:

Sir T. Clifford Allbutt, K.C.B., Regius Professor of Physics at the University of Cambridge.

William Archer.

Sir Thomas Barlow, Bart., K.C.V.O., President of the Royal College of Physicians.

Arnold Bennett.

Robert Blatchford.

Muirhead Bone.

Rev. R. J. Campbell.

G. K. Chesterton.

Sir William Crookes.

Sir Francis Darwin.

9

Sir Arthur Conan Doyle.

Sir James G. Frazer, author of *The Golden Bough*.

The Right Hon. Sir Edward Fry, G.C.B.

John Galsworthy.

G. P. Gooch, Editor of *Official Documents of the War* and the *Contemporary Review*.

A. G. Gardiner, Editor of the *Daily News*.

Mrs. John Richard Green, widow of the historian.

Maurice Hewlett.

Silas K. Hocking.

The Rev. Robert F. Horton, President of The National Free Church Council.

Jerome K. Jerome.

Robert Lynd.

Sylvia Lynd.

John Masefield.

H. W. Massingham, Editor of *The Nation*.

Sir William Robertson Nicoll, Editor of the *British Weekly*.

Sir Sydney Oliver, K.C.M.G.

The Rev. Thomas Phillips, President of the Baptist Union.

C. P. Scott, Editor of the *Manchester Guardian*.

Clement Shorter, Editor of *The Sphere*.

Ben Tillett, the Labour Leader.

Beatrice and Sidney Webb, founders of the Fabian Society.

The Right Rev. the Bishop of Winchester.

Israel Zangwill.

Behind the scenes the Archbishop of Canterbury, though for technical reasons he did not sign the petition, made a personal appeal to the Prime Minister.

In America the movement for a reprieve was strongly supported by Senator Henry Cabot Lodge, one of the most distinguished representatives of New England and a close friend of Sir Cecil Spring-Rice, who also supported the petition. It was followed by a resolution, passed by the Senate of the United States and submitted to the British Foreign Office with a strong plea for clemency.[1]

Casement's life had largely been spent, and his health broken, in unselfish unremitting service to suffering humanity in Africa and the Putumayo.

At the precise psychological moment, however, for the defeat of the petitions and to prevent Casement being regarded in Ireland as a patriot-martyr, a "diary" recording unnatural offences was alleged to have been found among his effects. On the advice of Sir Ernley Blackwell (the legal adviser to the Home Office) officially typed copies and photostatic extracts were circulated behind the scenes of the trial, through London clubs, among Members of Parliament and others, who might be thought to influence public opinion.

The methods used were admittedly disgraceful, and for forty years now there has been a growing suspicion that this "diary" is as wicked a forgery as the notorious Pigott letters in the Parnell case.

My name has been constantly used, for forty years now, as one of those who vouched for the authenticity of the alleged "diary" (or "diaries", according to taste).

Nineteen years ago W. B. Yeats in a poem challenged me to desert what he called the side of the forger and the perjurer, and "speak your bit in public that some amends be made". In the open letter[2] which I wrote to him at the time

---

[1] *Life and Letters of Walter H. Page*, by Burton Hendrick.
[2] The correspondence was printed in full in my book *Two Worlds for Memory*.

and which was published on March 3rd, 1937, in *The Irish Press*, I suggested that a committee of four experts should be chosen to examine the original alleged "diary". The suggestion, though since that day it has been most urgently renewed by others, has met with nothing but evasions. But examination of all the evidence available reveals one damning fact: In every attempt that has been made to substantiate the charges against Casement's moral character, there turns out to be something distorted, untrue, and in some cases obviously manipulated or given a false colouring by change of phrase.

I am now convinced that what in perfectly good faith I accepted in 1916 was imposed upon me, as it was imposed upon many others. A list of those to whom the typed copies were shown includes Walter Hines Page (the American Ambassador), Ben Allen of the Associated Press, Michael Collins, Hensley Henson (afterwards Bishop of Durham), President Wilson and King George V.

In the dreadful campaign against a man whom even Scotland Yard described as an idealist, my name has been so frequently quoted that I feel it incumbent on me to do, in a fuller form, what W. B. Yeats asked me to do. For some years now the ghost of Roger Casement has been beating on my own door.

An article in the *New Statesman* on March 31st, 1956, referred to me, quite correctly, as one of the many to whom an officially typed copy had been *shown*—an unsolicited and quite unexpected exhibit. In a letter to the *New Statesman* published on April 28th, 1956, I agreed with the writer of the article that the official use of those documents was blackguardly, and I expressed my belief that the evidence, accumulating over a long period of years, had branded them as fraudulent.

On May 3rd, 1956, in an Adjournment Debate, questions about the authenticity of the "diaries" were asked in the House of Commons by the Unionist Member for Belfast, Lieut.-Col. Montgomery Hyde, and my name was again mentioned, this time incorrectly, as one of those who had *exhibited* the diaries. I give here the relevant passages from the *Hansard Report*, as they conveniently summarize the present state of the affair:

"MR. MONTGOMERY HYDE (Belfast, North): I am not raising the case of the Roger Casement papers in any partisan spirit. I am not concerned whether Casement was a national hero or a traitor or a misguided idealist, but merely with the question of whether certain diaries and other notebooks attributed to him are genuine or false. These diaries are understood to be preserved in the so-called 'Black Museum' of Scotland Yard.

"Copies of this material were circulated at the time of Casement's trial in 1916, and they played a significant part in the events leading up to his execution. These documents purported to show that Casement was a homosexual, and they had the effect of alienating the sympathies of a number of individuals who would otherwise have supported the movement for his reprieve.

"People who knew Casement, including some still living, amongst them Mr. William Cadbury the well-known Quaker, take the view that these documents are spurious. I understand that Mr. Cadbury has recently communicated this view to the Hon. Member for Ladywood (Mr. V. Yates). Mr. Cadbury, and others like him, think that these documents, or at any rate certain portions of them, are the diaries of a scoundrel and pervert named Armando Normand, whom Casement came across when investigating the rubber atrocities in the Putumayo for the Foreign Office, and that Casement translated these diaries from the Spanish in which they were originally written and kept a copy in his own handwriting, as he considered that they could not be entrusted to a typist.

"The subject has come into prominence lately through two publications. One of these is a book called *The Eyes of the Navy* by a former member of this House, Admiral Sir William James. That book deals with the life of Sir Reginald Hall, who was in charge of Naval Intelligence at the Admiralty in the First World War, and, as such, was entrusted with the interception and decoding of German naval messages, including those about Casement's activities in Germany and his last ill-fated voyage in a U-boat to the Irish coast. According to the author of that book it was Captain Hall, as he then was, who was mainly responsible for the surreptitious circulation of extracts from the diaries, having previously received the text from Sir Basil Thomson, at that time Assistant-Commissioner of Police and head of the C.I.D.

"The other book is a new life of Casement by the well-known journalist, Mr. René MacColl. Mr. MacColl, as he states in his book, wrote to my Right Hon. and gallant Friend the Home Secretary asking, not to see the diaries but merely whether their existence could be officially confirmed. Mr. MacColl was informed that my right hon. and gallant Friend was unable to supply him with any information on the matter. This has been the stock official answer for many years, certainly since 1930, and it has recently been given to the hon. Member for South Ayrshire (Mr. Emrys Hughes) and myself.

"In 1930, Professor Denis Gwynn, who was engaged on a biography of Casement, asked to see the diaries and referred to a description of them which had been given by Sir Basil Thomson in one of his books. The then Home Secretary, Mr. J. R. Clynes, replied:

" 'On inquiry, I find that it was decided long ago not to make any official statement as to the existence or non-existence of these diaries. I have carefully considered that rule, and there seem to me to be very good reasons why in the public interest it is desirable not to break the official silence.'

"Mr. Clynes did not state what these reasons were, but on the subject of Sir Basil Thomson he added:

" 'You mention that reference to these diaries has been made by Sir Basil Thomson, but any such statements were completely unauthorized.'

"Five years before that, in 1925, another journalist, Mr. Singleton-Gates, who had had access to typed copies of the diaries, announced that he was publishing a book based on the diaries. He was sent for by the then Home Secretary, Sir William Joynson-Hicks, and was threatened with the application of the Official Secrets Act if he persisted in his intentions to publish his book. He was also seen by the authorities in Scotland Yard. In a letter to the *Evening Standard* dated 18th April, 1956, Mr. Singleton-Gates wrote:

15

" 'A few days later I was seen at Scotland Yard by the chief of the C.I.D., Sir Wyndham Childs, whose main concern was whether I had seen the documents during his régime. He confirmed the existence of the diaries and copies. He went much further, though I had never doubted the authenticity of the diaries.'

"I think it can be inferred from that statement that Mr. Singleton-Gates actually saw the originals of these diaries.

"On the other hand, it has been suggested that the diaries are deliberately faked by Sir Basil Thomson, who intermingled some Casement genuine diaries with the obscene Putumayo diaries of Armando Normand. Sir Basil Thomson's family, with whom I have been in touch, are naturally distressed by this accusation, which they regard as unfounded, and they are anxious to have his name cleared.

"Sir Basil Thomson has given four accounts of how the diaries were discovered, and subsequently used. They differ on minor points, but all agree that they were found by the police in one of Casement's trunks as a result of a search of his old lodgings some months before his arrest, while he was still in Germany.[1]

"There is no doubt from the published writings of Sir Basil Thomson that he believed the diaries to be genuine, as indeed did everybody else to whom photographs of several of the pages and typed extracts were shown. The then Attorney-General, Sir F. E. Smith, later Lord Birkenhead, was anxious that the defence should, if it wished, use these diaries as evidence of the possible insanity of Casement, but Casement's leading defence Counsel, Serjeant Sullivan,

[1] This is quite incorrect. There are extremely grave discrepancies in his various accounts on this very point. See Chapter IX.

16

refused to agree or even to look at them at the trial to support
such a plea. The material was also shown by Sir Basil
Thomson to the then legal adviser to the Home Office, the
late Sir Ernley Blackwell.

"In his autobiography, published in 1939, Sir Basil
Thomson quoted a passage from his own diary, the entry
being a few days after Casement's appeal had been dismissed. It is dated Saturday, 25th July, 1916, and is as
follows:

" 'Saturday, July 22, 1916. . . . Yesterday . . . I . . .
saw Sir Ernley Blackwell who read me his memorandum
to the Cabinet on the execution of Casement. It was very
well written. He had incorporated in it all the information
that I had collected and which was circulated on Wednesday. The waverers accepted the position that the law
was to take its course, but on Thursday Lord Crewe circulated a letter from Eva Gore-Booth, Countess Mark-
iewicz's sister, alleging that Casement's object in coming
over was to stop the rebellion. Blackwell confessed that he
did not know, with such a weak Cabinet, what the result
would be.'

"A copy of the Memorandum of 17th July, 1916, has
come into my possession, and it might be of interest to the
House if I read it:

" 'Exercise of the Prerogative on the ground of Insanity.'
" 'Casement's diary and his ledger entries covering
many pages of closely typed matter, show that he has for
years been addicted to the grossest sodomitical practices.

" 'Of late years he seems to have completed the full cycle of sexual degeneracy, and from a pervert, has become an invert—a 'woman' or pathic who derives his satisfaction from attracting men and inducing them to use him. The point is worth nothing, for the Attorney-General has given Sir E. Grey the impression that Casement's own account of the frequency of his performances was incredible and of itself suggested that he was labouring under hallucination in this respect. I think that this idea may be dismissed. I believe that the diaries are a faithful and accurate record of his acts, thoughts and feelings just as they occurred and presented themselves to him. . . . No one who has read Casement's report to the Foreign Office on the Putumayo atrocities (at a time when his sexual offences were of daily occurrence), his speech from the dock . . . his private letters to friends . . . could doubt for a moment that Casement, intellectually, at any rate, is very far removed from anything that could properly be described as insanity.

" 'His excesses may have warped his judgment and in themselves they are of course evidence of disordered sexual instincts, but they have not in my opinion any relevance in consideration of his crime, such as drunkenness, sexual excesses, jealousy, revenge, provocation, etc., have in the case of crimes of violence. . . .'

"In a second memorandum, Blackwell concludes:

" 'So far as I can judge, it would be far wiser from every point of view, to allow the law to take its course *and by judicious means to use these diaries to prevent Casement from attaining martyrdom.*'

18

"That is precisely what happened. Those who were shown the typed copies or photographs included Dr. Davidson, Archbishop of Canterbury; Dr. Henson, Bishop of Durham, and the Irish Nationalist leader John Redmond. They all refused to sign a petition for Casement's reprieve in consequence. The copies were also shown to President Wilson, who got them from the U.S. Ambassador, Mr. Page, who in turn got them from Sir Basil Thomson. Another American, Mr. Ben Allen of Associated Press News Service, was shown the original by Hall, and offered copies for cabling to New York. He asked if he could confront Casement with them in prison, but this request was repeatedly refused.

"I have here a letter from Mr. Allen, who is still alive, dated 7th March, 1956, in which he says:

" 'My only concern when I was solicited by Hall to cable the story of the alleged diary to New York was to pay due heed to the ethical code of the Associated Press which prevented me from handling the story until I had verified every pertinent fact connected with it. That was the only discussion I had with Hall—my insistence that I take the copy of the diary to Casement to get his side of the story. His repeated refusal convinced me that there was something back of it that he dared not disclose. Now I am sure of it. To me, the purpose is obvious now; to blacken Casement's character so that the United States would not ask for his reprieve.'

"These stories reached Casement in the condemned cell and he immediately denied them to his solicitor, Mr. Gavan Duffy. It is about time that this matter was cleared up. No one wants to see the diaries published, but I would suggest to my hon. Friend that a small committee of experts might be appointed, say two drawn from Ireland and two from this country, to examine the diaries and any relevant available evidence. They could do that and give an opinion whether or not they really are Casement's. Such an inquiry, incidentally, would also serve the purpose of establishing Sir Basil Thomson's *bona fides* or otherwise.

"The question of these diaries has excited and will continue to excite public interest, particularly in Ireland. It inspired the Irish poet, W. B. Yeats, to write a poem of which each verse ends with the line:

" 'The ghost of Roger Casement
Is beating on the door.'

"I can assure my hon. Friend that his ghost will continue to beat on the door of his office until he allows these diaries to be seen by reliable experts. Only then will it be possible to resolve all doubts about this matter once and for all, and I invite him to take that step.

"MR. EMRYS HUGHES (South Ayrshire): I cannot see why the Home Office does not accede to the very reasonable request made by the hon. Member for Belfast, North (Mr. Hyde). This appears to be a dirty little secret of the Home Office, kept in some safe after forty years, and the Home Office appears to be as anxious to hide the documents now as it was to exhibit them in 1916. So long as this attitude is adopted by the Home Office, so long will there be doubt in Ireland—a doubt which this country will share. I cannot see any reason why the documents should not be handed over to experts. . . .

"THE JOINT UNDER-SECRETARY OF STATE FOR THE HOME DEPARTMENT (MR. W. F. DEEDES): My hon. Friend the Member for Belfast, North (Mr. Hyde), has given a very detailed account of the events surrounding and subsequent to the execution of Sir Roger Casement, and I am quite sure that he does not expect me to comment in detail upon the version which he has given. I think I should do best if I addressed myself to his main request, which has been reinforced by the hon. Member for South Ayrshire (Mr. Emrys Hughes), that there should be an outside examination of these papers. It would be fairest if I went on to say, straight away, that I think it unlikely that I shall be able to give him such satisfaction in his quest.

"It is always rather disagreeable for all the parties involved to have to be stubbornly uncommunicative at this Dispatch Box, particularly upon a matter which has aroused, and continues to arouse, so much curiosity. Before to-day the Home Office has been accused of being secretive, obscurantist and even blackguardly in its attitude about this matter. I do not think that such charges are merited, nor, in this instance, are they original. We are faced with the difficulty, as in many matters affecting the Home Secretary, that any effective attempt to justify secrecy or silence about this must involve breaking that silence——

"MR. LESLIE HALE (Oldham, West): But the diaries have been exhibited.

"MR. DEEDES:—and revealing evidence and committing, without any good reason at this moment, a complete breach of the policy which, I believe, has been rightly upheld for many years.

"MR. HALE: We should not complain about the secrecy

21

had there been secrecy from the start. Then no one would have complained at all. The complaint is that these documents were exhibited round the House while hon. Members were awaiting the execution of Casement. Is that true or not? And if they were, why cannot they be exhibited now?

"MR. DEEDES: If the hon. Member will allow me to proceed, we shall come to that question.

"I said that I believed that the policy had been a right one. I have studied the correspondence over the years on this issue with great care. My hon. Friend is not the first to seek information about the Roger Casement papers. He is the last of a long line extending over a quarter of a century, and Home Secretaries of both parties have consistently refused to give any information to anyone. They have resisted pressure from many sources, some highly responsible, some not so responsible. But the plea made to the Home Secretary has generally had the same foundation, and my hon. Friend has indicated it to-night.

"I will attempt to put it as fairly as I can. The allegations are that the Government used diaries, real, copied or deliberately forged, to smear Casement and influence opinion in America; that such infamous allegations should be met by publishing the diaries and that continued silence is unfair——

"MR. HALE: It was said by Member after Member in 1916.

"MR DEEDES:—and gives substance to the allegations. I think that is a fair summary of the case. This most seductive argument is used whenever any new book on the subject appears, and there have been a good many books.

"It is a difficult argument for any Government to meet, but in each case it has been resisted and to-night my hon.

Friend has not advanced any fresh ground for saying that at this moment my right hon. and gallant Friend should submit to it. Whenever any controversialist stirs up the dust on this or any like issue we are told that only a complete disclosure will lay the dust. I do not think that is an argument which bears examination, and I will try to explain why. The important point was made the other day by, I believe, the right hon. Member for Grimsby (Mr. Younger), that the most respectable precedents should be reviewed from time to time, and I can give my hon. Friend the assurance that that is done and that there are no cobwebs on this particular file.

"MR. HALE: Does the Parliamentary Secretary deny that hon. Member after hon. Member of this House has recorded in his reminiscences that he was shown copies of the documents before Casement was shot——

"MR. HUGH DELARGY (Thurrock): He was hanged.

"MR. HALE: I thought he was shot——

"MR. DELARGY: He was hanged.

"MR. HALE:—and that some refused to intervene because they had seen documents which they believed came from the Home Secretary? Where did they come from?

"MR. EMRYS HUGHES: Alfred Noyes.

"MR. DEEDES: As I was saying, we do from time to time review the decision which has been taken by successive Home Secretaries. It is not taken for granted and I can assure my hon. Friend that a review has been carried out on this occasion. But where there exist good general grounds for not departing from the policy of silence on this issue, I think that the onus lies on those who seek to change it to bring forward strong reasons for changing it at this moment.

"The attitude of the Home Office is not that of mere secretiveness. Official papers are not normally disclosed until a considerable time has elapsed. The practice is now to deposit papers in the Public Record Office after 50 years, and those on capital cases are not open to inspection. It is asked, 'Is this in the interest of historical truth?' It has often been necessary to allow a passage of time before uncovering the whole truth about historical events. That is a fact which genuine historians accept.

"Although the rule is at times very irksome, it has sound foundations, and one relevant to this case is that as time elapses and generation succeeds generation, the passion goes out of political controversy. This convention was not invented by the Home Office for Casement. But the Casement case is a good example of the convention's soundness. The events are still a source of passionate partisanship. Whatever the truth, and however we were to reveal it, the inevitable consequence would be to stimulate and not to mollify those passions. Moreover, any disclosure about this tragedy, whether it be the diaries do or do not exist, are genuine or otherwise, must lead to renewed controversy about Casement's character and his part in the events which occurred.

"He landed in Kerry on Good Friday, 1916, and while these events are beyond the recollection of my generation, and are growing dim in the recollection of an older generation, they are remembered in Ireland with pride and bitterness. Whatever we said about this now would incite, first, curiosity, then a demand for more evidence, and finally inevitably a good deal of bitter controversy. The embers would most certainly be fanned into flame—and to what good? To provide material for a fresh research (HON.

MEMBERS: 'Truth')—for Truth, if you like. Truth might be found to be many-sided. To vindicate those concerned 40 years ago? Or to vindicate Casement? That was the point raised by one hon. member.

"This brings us to the point of whether the diaries were genuine. The latest version quoted by my hon. Friend is, I gather, that they are. So it is said that there would be no harm in confirming it. But on the contrary, if it were true and we were to confirm it, we would be giving from official sources information detrimental to the character of a man who had been a prisoner. It is an important principle that the Home Office does not do that, and it is doubly important when the prisoner has paid the extreme penalty.

"I foresaw the arguments which would be raised against it. What right has the Home Office to decide what is fit for publication? I think that the Home Office has a very heavy responsibility, more serious than anyone else. I do not take the decisions for the last 25 years by Home Secretaries, or even the 50-year rule, as conclusive. I think there is much more to it than that, and I ask the hon. Gentlemen to pay attention to this point.

"There is a fundamental principle that *no official disclosure should make it possible for anyone further to blacken the memory of a man who has been imprisoned and hanged.* I put that first. There is a second which I think will commend itself to the House, that where to break silence may only stimulate memories bitter and bloody then it is better to remain silent. *The day may come when these considerations will either not apply, or will apply with a great deal less force than they do to-day. It will then be for the Home Secretary of that time to determine whether or not the time has arrived to make the disclosure for which my hon. Friend asks.*

"MR. HUGH DELARGY (Thurrock): We have just heard about the weakest and the most ill-informed reply that I have ever heard in an Adjournment debate. The Joint-Under-Secretary of State for the Home Department speaks about his refusal to publish the diaries. That was not asked for. What was asked for was that a small committee of experts, some of them in the confidence of the Irish people, should be allowed to examine these documents if they exist, and then to say, without necessarily divulging their contents, whether or not the documents are genuine personal records. That is all that is asked for.

"The Joint Under-Secretary is talking about a complete disclosure. No one has asked for that. What has been asked for is a small thing. The hon. Gentleman takes refuge in trying, as he says, to defend the memory of Casement, when in fact Casement's memory was blackened in order that he should be the more conveniently hanged. . . ."

On May 17th, 1956, *The Times* published a letter from me in which I said:

"I have just seen *Hansard* for May 3rd. According to this, during the discussion on the Casement papers a Member, Mr. Emrys Hughes, stated that I was responsible for the circulation of the documents from the Home Office which caused people to refrain from signing the petition for Casement's reprieve.

"This is absolutely false and it is also an illustration of the wrong that is being done to private individuals by the disgraceful conduct of the Home Office.

"In 1916, when I was doing some work in the News Department of the Foreign Office, a copy of the alleged 'diary' was placed upon my desk.[1] It was a typed not a photographic copy as Mr. MacColl states in his book. *It was left with me for a few minutes* and was then somewhat hastily withdrawn. *It was never in my possession.* I was merely one of the many to whom it was shown (as we now know) on the disgraceful recommendation of the legal adviser to the Home Office [Sir Ernley Blackwell].

"In my first revulsion of disgust at the thing that had been shown to me I naturally made the expected comment and this was incorporated as a brief paragraph in an article which was sent out, not by me but by the News Department, for propaganda purposes. This was my sole connection with the documents and for nearly forty years now I have been reviled in a considerable section of the Irish press and in the book entitled *The Forged Diaries of Roger Casement*. There was a particularly savage outburst on my seventieth birthday.

"In 1916 I had no doubt at all of the good faith of the Home Office. I had no idea at the time that the documents had been repeatedly offered to the Associated Press and were rejected on ethical grounds because authentication had been repeatedly refused. There could have been no possible excuse for this refusal if the documents were genuine, for at the time copies were being actively circulated.

"May I therefore say here that there has been an accumulation of evidence, not least in the evasiveness of the Home Office itself, which has forced me to the conclusion that the documents are spurious. The spokesman of the Home Office complains that the word 'blackguardly' as applied to

[1] By Stephen Gaselee (afterwards Sir Stephen Gaselee, K.C.M.G., Librarian of the Foreign Office).

27

the conduct of his department is unmerited and 'not original'. But, as the Prime Minister said recently, it is difficult to find new words for truths which are permanent. May I therefore explain to Mr. Deedes why the word is justifiable?

"(i) It is against the first principles of justice and indeed in some cases it is a criminal offence to circulate surreptitious charges against a man who is on trial, even though in the phrase of the legal adviser to the Home Office the means used are 'judicious'.

"(ii) It is gross hypocrisy to pretend that authentication is now refused to protect the reputation of Casement from those to whom the Home Office deliberately disclosed the spurious documents for the express purpose of preventing 'hero worship' and it is an offence against those private individuals whom they misled and let down.

"(iii) It is something worse than Pecksniffian for the Home Office to insinuate that, while protecting the reputation of Casement, disclosure of what it is hiding would blacken his character even more.

.   .   .   .   .

"The only right course would be for the Home Office to admit that in the heat of the war things were done for which there is now no excuse. Irish feeling will only be exacerbated by its present policy. However misguided Casement may have been in thinking that the gun-running exploits of F. E. Smith, who after all threatened the British Government with civil war in Ulster, were an excuse for the rather pitiful attempt at gun-running in Southern Ireland, his character should be cleared of these charges.

"The English, in fact, would have an opportunity of winning the heart of Ireland if they acceded to the request of the many thousands who wish that his body should be returned to his native country. I believe that if the British Government behave chivalrously in this matter they would have their reward in history."

Shortly after this three statements were circulated which, if they were true, would discourage further requests for authentication.

The first, attributed to "responsible persons" (unnamed), was that the original documents had been destroyed.

But on May 3rd, 1956, as we have seen in the passage from *Hansard*, the Parliamentary Representative of the Home Office, in the House of Commons, answering the Unionist Member for Belfast, not only gave his reasons for not disclosing the documents at the moment, but enlarged upon the manner of their safe-keeping and the prospect of their being subjected to expert examination at a future date when political passions had subsided.

One can hardly believe that the Parliamentary Representative of the Home Office was either acting a lie, implying a lie or directly telling a lie about the possibility of that "disclosure", and what a little earlier he called "revealing the evidence". It must have been the revelation of the original documents ("for which my hon. Friend asks"), not a disclosure of an empty safe, for that would "blacken" nobody, the thing which he said might ensue. If, however, he was telling the truth, the documents must have been in existence on May 3rd, 1956.

But if the responsible persons (unnamed) were also speaking the truth, the documents must have been destroyed since May 3rd, 1956 (the date on which the representative of the Home Office acknowledged their existence). Yet this panic measure, when the pressure for expert examination became almost too strong to resist, in the face of the inquiries that were being made in the House of Commons and elsewhere, would be the most damning self-indictment of all.

We may take it, therefore, that the Home Office was not acting or implying a lie, and that the original documents do most certainly exist. Apparently they may still be whispered about but not seen; for an officially typed copy was shown to Lieut.-Col. Montgomery Hyde within a week or two of my letter to *The Times*.

The second statement, based on an interview in 1954 between Mr. René MacColl and Casement's aged counsel, Serjeant Sullivan, was that Casement in prison had confessed to Serjeant Sullivan that he had been guilty of the unnatural offences recorded in the "diary" (or "diaries"). Pressed for an explanation, Serjeant Sullivan flatly contradicted the story that Casement had confessed to him, and in a letter to *The Irish Times* said that *Casement told me nothing about the diaries or about himself*.

Serjeant Sullivan, who is now at an advanced age, made other statements quite incompatible with each other and with the direct evidence of two other eminent lawyers who acted on Casement's behalf. This peculiar feature of the case will be fully discussed in a subsequent chapter.

A third statement, also calculated to discourage further inquiries, has been in circulation for some time, that the Irish Government had been convinced long ago of the authenticity of the diaries. In view of the emphatic official denials in the Irish Parliament during 1956, it is scarcely necessary to deal with this matter further.

It has even been suggested that the Irish Government has entered into an agreement with the British Government to say nothing about the diaries. In reply to a Parliamentary question on the subject (Dail Reports, June 28th, 1956) the Minister for External Affairs, Mr. Cosgrave, replied:

"I have seen a published statement of the nature to which the Deputy refers. The Irish Government has not at any time entered into a concordat, or any other form of agreement, with the British Government concerning any aspect of the *alleged* 'Casement Diaries'."

Furthermore, the Irish Government has repeatedly asked that the body of Sir Roger Casement should be returned to his native land.

In all the statements discouraging authentication appears the same kind of distortion of truth which I encountered in 1916, when the one brief paragraph (mentioned in my letter to *The Times*) was published in America with false captions and even, as I learned years later, with additions, including the statement that I had "made search" to authenticate the diary—the very thing I was quite unable to do. These tactics are all the more unsavoury since, about the same time, the Associated Press representative was refusing on ethical grounds to be used for the same purpose.

CHAPTER II

THIS BOOK IS chiefly concerned with the manipulation of the diaries officially circulated behind the scenes of the trial. Legally, of course, they had no bearing on the charge for which Casement was later executed, but there can be no doubt that they were instrumental in deterring many public figures who would otherwise have pressed for a reprieve, in view of Casement's past reputation and the extenuating circumstances of his conduct. The crime of treason is so heinous that those who have forgotten the extraordinary political atmosphere of the time and place usually assume that Casement's guilt on the treason charge (which he admitted himself) had the base qualities usually, and rightly, associated with that word in normal circumstances. They allow this quite erroneous belief to confirm the moral charges against him.

The defence of Casement on the moral question has been greatly hampered by this assumption. It is therefore necessary to ask one or two plain questions.

These questions, which an English Jury at a time of war hysteria could hardly be expected to consider with impartiality, were put with great force by Casement's counsel at the time of the trial. They were most skilfully glossed over by the Attorney-General, as will be shown in a later chapter. They may now be submitted with some confidence to the judgment of any fair and chivalrous mind, not on any technical legal point, but simply as evidence that, if provocative circumstances ever alter cases, here were those circumstances and that provocation. They throw a flood of light upon the motives and actions of a man described by his friends as the very soul of honour. His counsel said:

"What are you to do when, after years of labour, your representatives may have won something that you yearned for, for many a long day [the Home Rule Bill], won it under the constitution, had it guaranteed by the King and the Commons, and you are informed that you should not possess it because those that disliked it were arming to resist the King and the Commons and to blow the statute off the books with powder? The Civil police could not protect you and the military force would perhaps prove inadequate for your support. You may lie down under it, but, if you are men, to arms; when all else fails, defend yourself."

The facts were given even more trenchantly by Winston Churchill in his condemnation of the gun-running in the north of Ireland:

"The party of the comfortable, the wealthy, the party of those who have most to gain by continuance of the existing social order, here they are committed to naked revolution, committed to a policy of armed violence and utter defiance of lawfully constituted authority, committed to tampering with the discipline of the Army and the Navy, committed to obstructing highways and telegraphs, to overpowering police, coastguards and customs officials, committed to smuggling in arms by moonlight, committed to the piratical seizure of ships, and to the unlawful imprisonment of the King's servants."

The Royal Commission on the Rebellion in Ireland confirmed, in cooler language, the fact that the formation of the southern Irish Volunteers was "the response of Nationalist Ireland to the Volunteer movement in Unionist Ulster."

Every visitor to what was once the Viceregal Lodge in Dublin, and is now the residence of the President of the Irish Republic, is confronted with Lavery's famous painting "The Trial of Sir Roger Casement". No Englishman who crosses that threshold and knows the background of the case can see that picture without some uneasiness of conscience on his own country's behalf.

As a complement to this picture there is another, a very vivid one in my mind. It offers a portion of that background necessary for any understanding of the case.

In 1914, at Rottingdean in Sussex, where I happened to be living at the time, Sir Edward Carson was escorted to his house there by a torchlight procession. It was in the midst of the agitation over the Home Rule Bill. Standing on the fringe of the crowd, I heard him make the famous speech in which he said: "If they want to take me they know where to find me." The dark, swarthy, saturnine face, as I saw it that night, left me with an impression of a grim personality, imbued with "courage never to submit or yield". Emotion ran so high at the time that when he waved what looked like a blackthorn cudgel, with a gesture that seemed to ask if the crowd were with him, almost every arm went up with the answering shout. So strong was the crowd infection that a forest of very ordinary English walking-sticks waved in the air before the Irish orator. He had made it quite clear, on the eve of the war with Germany, that he was prepared to wage civil war against the British Government with German arms, and if necessary with German military aid.

The bull-headed brass-hat attitude of "Casement was a traitor and there's an end of it" becomes sheer nonsense when one considers the manœuvres in 1914 of the two great

34

English political parties, the Liberals and the Conservatives, as well as those of the Irish party under Redmond. Nobody can understand the Casement affair who is unacquainted with the tragi-comic tangle of conflicting loyalties which forms its background.

Asquith, Prime Minister of the Liberal party which was then in power, having successfully got the Home Rule Bill through Parliament, was sending troops into North Ireland to enforce its application on a population which was threatening to fight rather than be driven out of the Union. Though he was what might be called agnostic with nonconformist prejudices, he preferred to force on "Protestant Ulster" a government which both he and Ulster believed to be diametrically opposed to their own principles. He was doing this not because he believed in the measure, but because he needed the votes of a large Irish party in the House of Commons. For this he blandly accepted the co-operation of Churchill, who at the time was a member of the Liberal Government and First Lord of the Admiralty.

Churchill approved and actively encouraged the steps taken to force Ulster out of the English Union against its will, even at the cost of fratricidal bloodshed. "There are worse things than bloodshed," he said in one of his speeches, "even on an extensive scale." This was all very well, and might have redounded to the orator's glory in a foreign war, but it was a fearful thing to say in contemplation of a war between two sections of the "United" Kingdom. He ignored his father's "Ulster will fight and Ulster will be right".

Balfour, the leader of the Conservative opposition, had described Churchill in the House of Commons as an *agent provocateur*, and had refused to withdraw the phrase. And

35

here we may quote, as against Balfour's description of Churchill, the following from the Journal of Lord Esher, "Keeper of the King's Archives", and "Liaison Between King and Army". Referring to a statement that the contest could only be fought out in Ireland he writes: "I said that 'Carson, a brave and resolute man, should be *encouraged to provoke* the contest at an early date ' " (Lord Esher's Journal, vol. 3 [the italics are mine]).

Balfour himself had defended the action of Carson and the oath of the Covenanters (some of whom signed it with their blood) by enunciating the principle that rebellion, even armed rebellion, against the Government of one's own country, was in certain circumstances justified. He did not define those cases, or touch upon the vital fact that in the present case, with the spectre of a war with Germany stark on the horizon, German arms and German aid on the most formidable scale were playing a part in the plans of his colleagues.

Carson and F. E. Smith, with the support of many Englishmen in high places, not only imported 30,000 rifles from Germany to fight the British Government, with Balfour's approval, but had issued a manifesto containing the following passage:

If the Home Rule Bill is passed, we shall consider ourselves absolutely justified in asking and rendering every assistance at the first opportunity to the greatest Protestant nation on earth, Germany, to come over and help us.

It must again be emphasized that this was on the very eve of the war with Germany, and that these suggestions could not have been made unless that war were already envisaged. They could not possibly have been made to any but an enemy power, and there is not the slightest doubt that this manifestation must at least have given "aid and comfort" to that enemy in its war plans. A statement to this effect was made by the Chairman of the Royal Commission on the Rebellion in Ireland, Lord Hardinge of Penshurst, K.G., P.C.[1]

Carson, though he was breaking the law openly and flagrantly, and declared that there was no law that he would not break, was in a stronger position than Asquith. It was not so easy to tackle Carson, with his 30,000 rifles and the big English political party behind him, as it was later savagely to turn the forces of the law, from all these conflicting sides, upon the broken and exhausted Casement, the whole of whose previous life had been spent in the service of mankind.

Gun-running from Hamburg, an invocation of German aid in the north; this, then, was the background against which an isolated, hyper-sensitive and too impulsive figure, Sir Roger Casement, made his ill-starred attempt at a counter-measure in southern Ireland. While the gun-running initiators of rebellion in the north moved forward to their glittering rewards and peerages, Roger Casement, only a few years after unmeasured praise had been poured upon him from the pulpit of Westminster Abbey, was found guilty, cheated out of the prerogative of mercy by surreptitous moral charges, died upon the gallows, and was buried in close proximity to the murderer Crippen.

[1] Ireland was in a state of internal unrest, almost verging on rebellion. This was known to Germany and it has always been assumed that the trouble in Ireland was one of the factors which Germany took into account in deciding on war. Report, p. 24.

CHAPTER III

A BRIEF ACCOUNT of Roger Casement's antecedents is necessary here. He was born on September 1st, 1864, at Sandycove, County Dublin, and after the death of his parents was taken to his uncle's house in County Antrim. He was then nine years old and went to school at the Ballymena Academy. At his uncle's house he read widely in books on Ireland and Irish history.

The suggestion made by F. E. Smith, Attorney-General, in his opening for the prosecution, that Casement's passionate feeling about the wrongs done to Ireland was the outcome of a sudden and malignant hatred of England, coincident with the outbreak of the war with Germany (and therefore had no moral or conscientious basis but was the effect of a treacherous nature) may be answered by the following facts from his personal background.

Casement's nationalism originated not in a sudden hatred of England, but in a life-long love for Ireland. His father was an ardent Nationalist, and resigned his commission in the army rather than take part in the eviction and destruction of the houses of the peasantry in County Sligo. In the movement for the "Liberation of Ireland" he joined with the Irish patriot John Mitchel, and when Mitchel was captured Casement's father was exiled. He aided Louis Kossuth in the war for Hungarian Independence.

Casement's father and Louis Kossuth, with Garibaldi and Mazzini, were regarded as heroic exemplars by Roger Casement. He would have subscribed to the tributes paid to Kossuth by two great English poets, Landor and Swinburne.

In 1881 Roger Casement took a post with the Elder Dempster Line, of which his uncle was a director, but in 1883, not content with office life, he sailed as Assistant Purser on one of the Company's ships to West Africa. Four years later he joined the American General Henry Sandford in an expedition to the Congo, a region in which the interest of the world had been aroused by the explorations of Livingstone and Stanley. The knowledge acquired on this journey and the lectures he subsequently gave established Casement as an authority on the subject, and in 1892 he was appointed travelling commissioner in the service of the Niger Coast Protectorate.

On leaving Nigeria in 1895 he was appointed Consul at Lourenço Marques. His administrative services were recognized as outstanding, and in 1898, on leaving Lourenço Marques, he was made Consul to the Portuguese possessions south of the gulf of Guinea. At the same time he was assigned the duties of Consul to the Gaboon and to the Congo Free State, and later also to the French Congo. For three more years he held these responsible positions and was gradually uncovering conditions in the Congo Free State which called for reform. It was about this time that a keen observer, Joseph Conrad, in a letter to R. B. Cunninghame Graham on December 26th, 1903, described him thus:

"I send two letters I had from a man named Casement, premising that I knew him first in the Congo. He is a Protestant Irishman, pious too. But so was Pizarro. For the rest I can assure you that he is a limpid personality. There is a touch of the conquistador in him too; for I have seen him start off into an unspeakable wilderness swinging a crook-handled stick for all weapon, with two bull-dogs, Paddy (white) and Biddy (brindle) at his heels, and a Loanda boy carrying a bundle for all company. A few months afterwards it so happened that I saw him come out again, a little leaner, a little browner, with his stick, dogs and Loanda boy, and quietly serene as though he had been for a stroll in the park. . . . He was, I believe, British consul in Beira, and lately seems to have been sent to the Congo again on some sort of mission by the British Government. I always thought some particle of Las Casas' soul had found refuge in his indomitable body. The letters will tell you the rest. I would help him but it is not in me. I am only a wretched novelist inventing wretched stories, and not even up to that miserable game; but your good blade, keen, flexible and straight, and sure like a good Toledo blade, would tell in the fray if you felt disposed to give a slash or two. He could tell you things! Things I've tried to forget, things I never did know. He has had as many years of Africa as I had months—almost."

Casement's investigation of conditions in the Congo (Conrad's *Heart of Darkness*) was to take a heavy toll of his strength. It covered many hundreds of miles through a country which, with its malaria, small-pox, yellow fever, sleeping sickness and other tropical diseases, might well be called the white man's grave, but he found a people mutilated, terrorized and decimated by the white agents of the Belgian rubber gang. In a man like Casement, hating cruelty or oppression, it needed an inflexible will and unbreakable courage to endure the sight of the horrible brutalities which he had to report.

He wrote to Mrs. John Richard Green (wife of the famous historian): "Up in those lonely Congo forests I found myself", but even here his heart was with his native country, for he continued: "The Congo will revive and flourish, the black millions again overflow the land—but who shall restore the destroyed Irish tongue?"

Here is a further proof of the utter falsehood of the suggestion made at his trial by the prosecution that Casement's nationalism, and his feeling about the treatment accorded to his country by England, was of sudden and malignant birth on the eve of a great war. It was in fact a noble and selfless thing, relating to the oppressed everywhere in the world. He wrote to a friend at some early date:

"There is so much to be done in the Congo matter that we shall need all our strength and the support of every friend of the weak and oppressed to help these poor persecuted beings in Central Africa. *It is a tyranny beyond conception—save only, perhaps, to an Irish mind alive to the horrors once daily enacted in his land.*"

What Casement sincerely felt about the things that had been done in Ireland may be compared, oddly enough, with the detached remark of Asquith who, when Prime Minister in 1912 and spending a holiday in Sicily, wrote to his wife Margot that the Sicilians were a semi-barbarous race who lived like the Irish and whose shocking roads made short work of the Rolls-Royce.[1]

It may be said incidentally that it was just this attitude which naturally aroused the anger of Casement on behalf of his own country. Compare the above for thought and feeling with what Casement wrote:

[1] *Mutiny at the Curragh*, by A. P. Ryan.

"There is so much to do here in Ireland that sometimes my heart faints when I think of the Congo and all its claims upon me, but I cannot even, for the sake of my own dear country, forget the poor people out there.

"And that is the way, I am sure, the claim of the Congo people must appeal to every sincere and genuine Irish native; the more we love our land and wish to help our people the more keenly we feel we cannot turn a deaf ear to suffering and injustice in any part of the world.

"I am quite sure that if I had not been an Irishman and an ardent believer in the nationality and rights of Ireland I should have passed through those Congo scenes of suffering humanity with a cold or at any rate so reserved a heart, that I should never have committed myself as I did to assume an attitude of insistence so uncompromising that the doubts of my chiefs were swept away."

These statements are of the utmost importance, for they completely destroy the suggestions of the Attorney-General mentioned on a preceding page. To Casement all these things were part of one cause, the cause of humanity.

On December 11th, 1903, back in London, Casement handed his finished report to Lord Lansdowne, the Foreign Secretary. It was published in February, 1904, in the form of a White Paper, and the extreme importance attached to it by the Government may be gauged by the following letter:

"The Marquess of Lansdowne to His Majesty's Representatives at Paris, Berlin, Vienna, St. Petersburgh, Rome, Madrid, Constantinople, Brussels, The Hague, Copenhagen, Stockholm and Lisbon.

Foreign Office, February 12, 1904.

"Sir:

"I transmit to you, for communication to the Government to which you are accredited, a collection of papers, as marked in the margin, which relate to the present condition of affairs in the Independent State of the Congo.

"In handing these documents to the Minister for Foreign Affairs I request that you will call special attention to the Report by Mr. Casement, his Majesty's Consul at Boma, upon a recent visit to certain districts of the Upper Congo, and that you will at the same time inquire when an answer may be expected to my despatch of the 8th August last.

"I am, &c.,

"(Signed) Lansdowne."

World-wide attention was thus drawn to the iniquities of the Belgian Congo administration. With incredible meanness Casement's accusers, after his death, have tried to belittle his work in the Congo. It is enough to say here that the Belgian Government itself sent out a Commission to investigate the truth of Casement's report, and that this Commission confirmed it in every detail—to the great discomfiture of the Belgian Government and King Leopold. Casement received official honours and was described again and again as a noble example of selfless idealism. The British Foreign Office was so completely satisfied with this confirmation by the Commission that in a communication to the Belgian Government it took for granted that the necessary reforms would be undertaken at once.

Casement anticipated this confirmation in a letter to a

43

friend in which, quite consistently with what he had said earlier, he wrote:

"*The Commission will confirm my report 'up to the hilt'. That will be a triumph indeed—and a triumph for Ireland too—as I may some day tell you. I knew well that if I told the truth about the devilish Congo conspiracy of robbers I should pay for it in my own future; but when I made up my mind to tell at all costs, it was the image of my poor old country stood first before my eyes. The whole thing had been done once to her—down to every detail—she, too, had been 'flung reward to the hounds'—and I felt that, an Irishman, come what might to myself, I should tell the whole truth. I burned my boats deliberately, and forced the F.O. either to repudiate me or back my report. And yet I knew quite well in the end I should have to go overboard, and I wrote that in September, 1903, the day I wrote to the Governor-General at Boma denouncing the whole infamous system, and so committing myself to 'no compromise'.*"

Whatever else may be said about these passages, they are not the words of a bad man, and they completely annihilate the opening charge of the prosecution. They were, also, in exact accord with the expression of that feeling by Irish parliamentary leaders, generation after generation. When Parnell was released in 1882 from the prison to which his defiance of what he called "English misrule" had brought him, he said to his sister: "What did you think they would do to me?" She replied: "I thought they would hang you." And Parnell answered: "That, too, may come."

All this is a part of the historical background without which the "duality" of Casement's political position cannot be fairly measured or understood.

In 1904 Casement founded the Congo Reform Association, of which Lord Cromer became chairman. Casement wrote:

44

"I don't want the Brussels gang of robbers to be able to say that the Congo Reform movement has been got up and engineered by Protestant missionaries. As a matter of fact it *originated* solely with me: I gave the idea to Morel whose generous heart and fiery soul at once responded—and our first recruit was as I say that good Irishman and good Catholic Lord ffrench. When I asked him to help me by lending his name he said he could not refuse—that it was the duty of a Christian, of every Christian who believed in his faith in God, to help such a call."

Early in 1904 Casement, with impaired health, returned to Ireland for a rest, and, in complete consistency with what he had said earlier about Ireland and its association with the cause of the oppressed everywhere in the world, he threw himself actively into the Nationalist movement. In November of that year he was appointed Consul to Lisbon. His work in Africa, as he expected, had aroused powerful enmities, and this was possibly why he was offered the new post. But, though it was more desirable from a worldly point of view, he was bitterly disappointed; he wished to return to Africa and continue his work there. Accordingly he asked to be seconded for sick leave without pay. This was granted and he returned to Ireland, where he worked for both the Congo Reform Association and the Nationalist movement.

His work for the Congo Reform Association had aroused so much attention all over the world that it was impossible to ignore him, and Sir Edward Grey wrote a cordial letter informing him that the Foreign Office would be very glad of his assistance and of his "return to the fold". He was asked, for intelligence purposes, to take up a consular appointment,

45

first in São Paulo, then in Panama, then in Para, and then in Rio de Janeiro.

It was here that he met Gerald Campbell (afterwards British High Commissioner in Canada and Minister in Washington), whose account of him again completely rebuts any suggestion that Casement's nationalism came to a head only in 1914.

"Casement came ashore, and we talked for a time before going back to his liner for lunch. Half-way out to the ship, the villainous Brazilian boatmen who were rowing us out suddenly rested on their oars, and as was their wont, tried to hold us up for more money than the price already agreed on. But by then Casement was launched on a tremendous monologue about Irish Home Rule and nothing could stem the flood. For a while the boatmen tried to shout him down but it was impossible. Finally they gave up in disgust and we continued on our way, with Casement still going strong on Ireland."

This passage, cited by Rene MacColl, depicts a humourous aspect of the consistent character who, in his generously romantic youthful poems, glorified Wolfe Tone in almost the same breath as he pleaded for the return of the Elgin Marbles to Athens.

CHAPTER IV

Casement's appointments took him by stages into a problem as revolting as that of the Congo—the atrocities of the Putumayo.

When in 1908 he was made Consul-General at Rio de Janeiro there were rumours about the scandalous treatment of the natives by a powerful rubber company in the Putumayo River region. Many were natives of Barbados and were British subjects. The Company responsible was registered in England as the Peruvian Amazon Rubber Company, with offices in London. The Putumayo River is a remote tributary of the Amazon, about 500 miles long, and the Putumayo basin lies among trackless jungles. Conditions there, according to rumour, were horribly like those against which Casement had fought in the Congo.

He first satisfied himself that these rumours were based on fact, and then on April 4th he sailed for home. There he consulted the Foreign Office, and in consequence of his urgent representations he was authorized by Sir Edward Grey to carry out an investigation in Putumayo. He arrived in Brazil in August, 1910, and reached Iquitos, a village in the interior, on the 31st. He was accompanied by five Commissioners who were appointed by the Peruvian Amazon Company, against which the charges were being brought. These were Col. the Hon. R. N. Bertie, C.B., H. L. Barnes, a tropical husbandry expert; W. Fox, a rubber expert; E. S. Bell, a merchant; and H. K. Gielgud, the

47

General Secretary and Manager of the Company. It is inconceivable that if the offences attributed to Casement in the spurious diaries really occurred "daily" at this very time, there should not have been the slightest whisper of it in such a company. It is doubly inconceivable when his work there, as in the case of the Congo investigation, had aroused so many fierce enmities. It is trebly inconceivable when his fellow investigators would naturally be anxious to exonerate their own Company from the guilt which Casement, and Casement alone, was trying to bring to light.

In Iquitos there was a British consul, and the party remained there for two weeks gathering evidence. There was no concealing the fact that the natives were shockingly exploited on a tremendous scale, and that white agents were responsible for flogging, torture and murder. One of the causes of this ferocity was that the white employees of the rubber firm were paid, in lieu of salary, a commission on the amount of rubber brought in by the natives, but cruelty for a purpose evidently led on to a diabolical delight in cruelty for its own sake.

Later Casement and the Commission proceeded up the Amazon to Putumayo.

The months Casement spent in the investigation might very well be described as "a season in Hell". His reports on the appalling crimes which were being committed there may justly be characterized as the most competent and conscientious ever presented to a Government Department. The proof is in their effect, for they moved the conscience of the civilized world. Behind their profound sincerity and humanitarian pity for the oppressed, there is an almost unmatched process of authentication, giving an exact picture

48

of the character and condition of the people about whom he writes.

It may be well here to lay before the reader some of the evidence which filled Casement with such passionate horror, as he records it in his report or as it was revealed to him by the deposition of eye-witnesses. The extracts are taken from his reports and correspondence, published by the British Government and "Presented to both Houses of Parliament by Command of His Majesty July 1912".

Extracts from Report of Consul General Casement, to Sir Edward Grey, dated March 17th, 1911.

". . . In 1905 the station of Matanzas or Andokes was the centre of a series of raids organized by the Colombian head of it, one Ramon Sanchez, at the time an agent of Arana Bros.[1] To this man the first contingent of Barbados men, British subjects . . . was handed over. They had been engaged by a partner of the firm, one Abel Alarco, and were brought to the Amazon by a Peruvian or Bolivian named Armando Normand, acting as interpreter in the pay of Arana. Normand was in charge of the station when I visited the country in 1910, and I found more than one of the Barbados men still in the Company's service. The testimony of these men, much of which will be found attached to this report in the statements made to me, was of the most atrocious description. . .

"The only Indians permitted the use of rifles were those young men who were being trained to oppress their country-men. . . These 'muchachos' were generally young Indians. In fairness to the Indian character, it must be pointed out that the worse crimes charged against the 'muchachos' . . .

[1] Founders of the Peruvian Amazon Rubber Co.

49

were committed under the direct orders of their white
lords. . .

"Perhaps the bravest and most resolute opponent the
murderers had encountered had met his death only a few
months, or even weeks, before my arrival in the district.
This was a Boras Cacique or 'capitan' named Katenere.
This man, young and strong, lived on the upper waters of
the Pama. . . My interpreter, Bishop, had seen this chief in
1907, when Normand had gone to find him in order to
induce him to work rubber. He had, from necessity no doubt,
consented to bring in rubber and had for some time worked
voluntarily for Normand, until, through bad treatment he,
like so many others, had fled. He had been captured later
on, along with his wife and some of his people, and confined
in the stocks of the Abisinia district, to undergo the taming
process. While thus himself a prisoner his wife . . . had been
publicly violated before his eyes by one of the highest agents
of the Syndicate, a Peruvian whose name and criminal
record were frequently brought forward in the course of my
inquiry. Katenere escaped, aided by an Indian girl, who
lifted off the top beam of the 'cepo' when no one was looking.
He not only got off but succeeded in capturing some Winchester rifles from 'muchachos' of the Abisinia district.
With these he armed others of his clan and thenceforward
waged an open war against the whites and all the Indians
who helped them or worked rubber for them. More than one
of them he shot and although a young man he became
renowned as a 'very bad Indian'. About May of 1909 he
found the white man who had so wronged him in the act of
compelling a party of Indians to wash their rubber at a
stream, and shot him dead. Thenceforward he became an

object of constant fear and expeditions were fitted out to catch or kill Katenere... It was on one of these missions that Filimene Vasquez and his party had gone in the summer of 1910 when he had 'left the road pretty'. They had captured the wife of Katenere and she was brought back to Abisinia to act as a decoy, her captors feeling that Katenere would come to look for his wife. This he had indeed done about the beginning of August or end of July, and it was while preparing to attack Abisinia in the dusk that he was shot by one of the young 'muchachos' of that station, as stated in the deposition of Evelyn Batson, which accompanies this report... The death of Katenere was greatly to be deplored...

"An Indian marriage is not a ceremony, but a choice sanctioned by the parents of the bride, and once a child or children result from the union there is rarely infidelity or separation. *The very conditions of Indian life, open and above-board, and every act of every day known to well-nigh every neighbour, precluded, I should say, very widespread sexual immorality before the coming of the white man. Certain it is that immoral intercourse among Indians, leading their natural lives, is rare, and as polygamy scarcely existed, only a few of the bigger men having more than one wife, the affection that grew up between the Indian man and his wife was very often sincere and deep-rooted, just as the love of parents for their children was.*

"The Indians often displayed a fortitude in the face of impending torture and death that speaks for itself of the excellence of some of their qualities. Thus it will be seen in the depositions accompanying this report how, on more than one occasion, men had refused to betray the hiding-place of fugitives under terrible threats of torture if they did not point out the retreat of the runaways. Normand is charged with having cut the arms and legs off a chief he captured and questioned, who preferred to suffer such a death to betraying the refuge of those who had fled. I learned of more than one case of the kind and have no doubt of the truth of the accusation against the white man as of the fortitude of the Indian. The tribes of the Putumayo in the hands of good men could be made into good men and women, useful and intelligent workers under an honest administration. Trained to be murderers, with the worst example men ever gave to men daily held up for imitation, with lust and greed and cruelty so often appealed to, I daily wondered that so much goodness still survived among the remnant we encountered. . .

"As far as possible I have given these men's statements in the men's words taken down at the time, but it would have required a shorthand writer and clerical assistance to have fully transcribed all that was stated at these lengthy examinations, some of which extended over many hours in the case of a single individual. Several of the depositions were later read over by me to the deponents and signed by them, but it was not always possible to adopt this course. As transmitted, the statements are as faithful records under the circumstances as it was possible for me to take down, of a mass of evidence that ran to great length and was offered sometimes in circumstances of great difficulty for the witness to state and often for me to record. . .

"In the course of our subsequent journey it became clearer every day that the statements of the Barbados men were only too well-founded, and before I left the Putumayo it was definitely established that their indictment could not be called in question."

52

From Casement's Report No. 10, dated March 21st, 1911,
to Sir Edward Grey:
"Statement of James Chase, native of Barbados, British
subject:

"About four months ago . . . he was sent on a commission
towards the Caqueta River. The expedition was commanded
by a man called Filomene Vasquez. . . . Soon after they
began their march in the morning they met in the path a
child—a little girl—who was said to be a daughter of
Katenere by another wife he once had. This child was quite
a young girl, some six or eight years of age. She was frightened at sight of the armed men, the Indians in chains and
tied up, and began to cry as they approached. Vasquez
at once ordered her head to be cut off. He knew it was
Katenere's child because Katenere's wife in their hands
told them so. There was no reason that Chase knew for the
crime, save that the child was crying. Her head was cut off
by a 'muchacho' . . . quite a young boy. They came on about
half an hour's march, leaving the decapitated body in the
path, and as one of the women prisoners they had was not
walking as fast as the rest Vasquez ordered a 'muchacho'
to cut her head off. This was done by the same boy Cherey in
the same way, he flinging the woman on the ground and
chopping her head off with several blows of his machete.
They left this body and severed head right in the path and
went on again. . . . About three-quarters of an hour's walk
further on one of the male Indian prisoners, a boy about 15
or 16, a boy who could work rubber, was lagging behind and
could not keep up with them as they were going very fast.
The Indian was hungry and probably weak. Vasquez
ordered his head to be cut off. . . . Cherey took hold of the

53

lad's long hair, threw him on the ground and cut his head off. . . Perhaps three-quarters of an hour's distance three of the Indian men who were weak from hunger and not able to walk fast could not keep up with them so Vasquez himself shot one and ordered Cherey, the 'muchacho', to shoot the other two. . . (Chase) was told that they had killed 13 Indians on this expedition."

Statement of Joshua Dyall ("one of the first contingent from Barbados"):

". . .'The second Indian you killed, who was he, and when?'

" 'He was in Andokes last year, in July. . . We killed him with a stick, not with a gun. Normand also, he and I beat him to death. We smashed up his——'

"He described how Normand compelled him to commit this crime. The Indian was thrown on the ground by Normand and himself, his legs distended apart, Normand holding the legs apart while he, Dyall, beat the man with a thick stick between the legs and so killed him. The interrogatory proceeded. 'You did that?'

" 'Yes, sir. Wait sir, you do not know how we do things here. If we do not do what the chief tells us he beats us.' "

Statement of Stanley Sealey, a native of Barbados, made on September 23rd, 1910, and on subsequent occasions:

". . . He . . with other Barbados men went on a commission from Abisinia under Jiménez. . . It was a journey to catch fugitive Indians who had fled from the rubber working. . . About 5 o'clock in the afternoon they . . caught an old woman in the path. Jiménez asked the old woman where the rest of the Indians were. Sealey states she was a bit frightened. She told him that the next day at 11 o'clock he would get to the house where some Indians were. She was an old woman not able to run. They did not tie her up. They went on with her, keeping her all night in camp until about two o'clock of the next day, and then Jiménez asked her 'Where is the house where are the Indians?' The old woman stood up and said nothing. She could not speak, she kept her eyes on the ground. Jiménez said to her: 'You were telling me lies yesterday, but now you have got to speak the truth.'

"With that he called his wife—he had an Indian woman, the woman who is still with him—and he said to his wife:

" 'Bring me that rope off my hammock.'

"She took the rope off and gave it to him, and with that he tied the old woman's hands behind her back. There were two trees standing just like that. . . He made an Indian cut a post to stretch between the two trees. Then he hauled the old woman up, her feet were not touching the ground at all. He said to one of the boys, a 'muchacho':

" 'Bring me some leaves—some dry leaves,' he said, and he put these under the feet of the old woman as she hung there, her feet about a foot or so above the ground; 'and he then take a box of matches out of his pocket and he light the dry leaves, and the old lady start to burn. Big bladders (blisters) I see on her skin up here' (he pointed to his thighs). 'All was burned; she was calling out. Well, sir, when I see that, sir, I said "Lord have mercy!" and I run ahead that I could not see her no more.'

" 'You did not go back?'

" 'I stayed a little ways off to where she was. I could hear him speaking. He say to one of the boys, "Loose her down now" and they loose her, but she was not dead. She lay on the ground—she was still calling out. He tell one of the Indians: "Now if this old woman is not able to walk, cut her head off," and the Indian did so—he cut her head off.'

" '. . . About four hours walk after we left the old woman we met two women. They had no house, they had run away. One had a child. Jiménez axed the one that had the child: "Where is these Indians that has run away?" She tell him that she don't know where they were. He tell her . . . that she was a liar. He tell his wife to tell her. His wife speaks Spanish too. . . He took the child from the woman and he gave it to an Indian, one of the Indians who had been collected to work rubber. "Cut this child's head off" he say, and he did so.'

" 'How did the Indian cut the child's head off?'

" 'He held it by the hair and chop its head off with a machete. It was a little child walking behind its mother.'

" 'Was it a boy or a girl?'

" 'It was a boy. He left the child and the head in the same place, everything there, on the path He went on then; he take the two women with him, but the woman was crying for her child. . .' " (Report pp. 80-81.)

On one occasion Casement accompanied one of the forced marches of Indians bringing rubber from distant places to La Chorrera, and did his best to help some of the weaker victims who fell out on the march. The report is vivid in detail and utterly selfless, but the emotional strain was far greater than it would have been to a man of less sensitive nature. In one passage towards the end the emotional strain does appear, though even here it is not of self-pity but of infinite compassion for others. In his private Putumayo diary (the authentic one now in the National Library of Ireland in Dublin) he writes:

"At night I am very tired. If only I could write shorthand. So much depends on noting at the time, leaving as little as possible to the memory. . . It is now 3.40 A.M. God guide me aright. God help me for the sake of these poor unhappy beings . . . my eye is getting very bad, and I have to do all my writing now with one eye, the right. My legs, wrists and arms are now a mass of sores from bites of most venomous sand-flies.

"One moves here in an atmosphere of crime, suspicion, lying and mistrust in the open, and in the background these revolting and dastardly murders of helpless people. If ever there was a helpless people on the face of the earth, it is these naked forest savages. Their very arms show the bloodlessness in their tired minds and gentle characters. . .

"The thing that we find here is carrion, a pestilence, a crime . . . a moral disease that religion and conscience and all that is upright in us should uncompromisingly condemn. . . . All native joy died in these woods when these Peruvian half-castes imposed on primitive people and gave them the bullet, the lash, the 'cepo' (stocks), and death by hunger, death by twenty forms of organized murder. They are not only flogged and chained up like wild beasts, hunted far and wide, but their dwellings are burned, their wives raped, and their children dragged away to slavery. God help the poor beings! Only He can help them!

"I will write no more to-day . . . I wonder where that Heavenly Power can be that has so far allowed these beautiful images of Himself to be thus defaced and shamed in the name of a great association of English gentlemen" (the Peruvian Amazon Company).

"I looked up from the verandah to the eastern sky and saw to my amazement an arc of light across the dark starless heaven. For the moment I did not realize what it was, then I saw it—a lunar rainbow, a perfect arc in the night, spanning the dark, curving from forested hill across the eastern heavens. I take it to be an omen, an omen of peace and augury of good that God is still there, looking down on the crimes and sins of men, hating the sin and loving the sinner. He will yet come to these poor beings, and out of the night a voice speaks."

It would be difficult to reconcile the tone of this, his real Putumayo diary, and also the circumstances in which it was written, with the daily offences alleged against Casement by the political enemies who determined to hang him. The passage is, however, in complete accord with his successful effort to establish a Franciscan Mission in the Putumayo, of which he wrote on July 16th, 1916, when he was under sentence of death in Pentonville Prison:

"I am indeed glad to hear the news from the Fathers there. The Franciscans were loved in Peru of old. It is a good thing to think of them there now in that dreary region. . . . Once I grieved at it, and thought I was sending them or asking for them to be sent out to bitter trial and disappointment, but it is not so, and they will see the fruit of their privations and of their self-sacrifice in the lives they save, and in the increase of life and happiness around them, to replace the old dreadful and mortal misery."

Casement returned to London in January, 1911, and made his report to Sir Edward Grey, but, in spite of the terrible

58

nature of the report, Government action was slow. Sir Edward Grey wrote him a warmly congratulatory note, telling him that he had been recommended for a knighthood.

This was not what Casement wanted, but it gave official recognition and the seal of Government approval to his report. This was exceedingly important to the cause he had at heart, and he naturally expressed his thanks for it in terms commensurate with its importance to that cause. This expression of thanks was afterwards most churlishly flung in his face as evidence of a sycophantic nature, by F. E. Smith, his political enemy, when as prosecuting attorney he was well on the way to the "glittering prize" of a peerage.[1]

Casement's personal feelings at the time were clearly expressed to his friends. It hurt and embarrassed him that honour should be bestowed on him while the reforms for which he fought were being delayed, and he chafed angrily against the usual inertia of Government Departments.

He had indeed already received a knighthood of a far higher order:

> Who lays on the sword?
> "I", said the Sun.
> "Before he has done
> I'll lay on the sword."

> Who'll shake his hand?
> "I", said the Fever,
> "And I'm no deceiver.
> I'll shake his hand."

[1] "The world continues to offer glittering prizes to those who have stout hearts and sharp swords. . . . Self-interest not only is, but must be and ought to be the mainspring of human conduct." F. E. Smith (Lord Birkenhead) in speech to students of Glasgow University (1923).

CHAPTER V

In 1912 E. D. Morel (who in 1904 had helped Casement to found the Congo Reform Association), wrote of him in the London *Daily News* of July 20th:

"A long, lean, swarthy Vandyck type of face, graven with power and withal great gentleness. An extraordinarily handsome and arresting face. There you have only a bald outline. There is something in the whole carriage and play of the man, a something which would stamp him as distinctive and apart in any assembly; a something which speaks of pure metal and a soul almost primitive both in simplicity and strength. I have never known such personal magnetism . . . It is not the physical gifts which are the primary cause, rather the mental unuttered conviction that is instantly formed that this man is the soul of honour."

That is a man's description of a man. Look on this picture by one who knew him intimately, and on that of the sorry figure given by Sir Ernley Blackwell (who did not know him) as a representation of Casement at this very time, and judge between them.

In early July Sir Edward Grey telegraphed to the British Minister at Lima: "Inform the Peruvian Minister for Foreign Affairs that I have read the report of your conversation with H.E., contained in your despatch of the 4th of May, and impress upon him that His Majesty's Government attach the greatest importance to Peru giving visible proof without further delay that she is determined to eradicate the present abuses in the Putumayo, and to arrest and bring before a proper Court the criminals implicated. Failing such proof they will have no alternative but to publish Sir Roger Casement's reports."

Language like this from Sir Edward Grey is a complete answer to the depreciations of those reports, which only began during the organized campaign of calumny.

But in spite of the above telegram and other urgent messages from Sir Edward Grey, no effective measures were taken by the Peruvian Government. It put up a considerable bluff by issuing some hundreds of warrants, of which only nine were executed. In fact, so many warrants were issued that the arrest of so many men in remote parts could not be carried out.

Casement returned to the Putumayo for the definite purpose of ascertaining what remedial measures had been taken. In the later belittling campaign it has been suggested that he was sent to prove that his earlier reports were not exaggerated. The suggestion is fantastic, for his earlier reports had been substantiated by the five representatives of the inculpated company who journeyed with him, and by the judicial representative of the Peruvian Government itself.

The British Government was using Casement's reports as the most powerful weapon to compel reform; and his detractors now ask us to suppose that the Foreign Office at that time wanted his own unaccompanied testimony to what had already been so fully substantiated. Let this lie then be nailed down and the plain truth be stated once for all—that on this occasion he went to the Putumayo for the express purpose of discovering whether the necessary reforms had been carried out, and if they had not he would, of course, enable the British Government to use the weapon with which he had already provided them.

He found that during his absence all the old evil conditions which his efforts had temporarily checked were being re-established. He reported this to Sir Edward Grey, with a most urgent appeal that the British Government should take more definite action. The responsibility, he argued, was British, since the entire rubber production on the Putumayo was being sent to England and was partly produced by the slave labour of British subjects. This again ensured him some powerful and unscrupulous enemies, since the rubber production had risen to a very large figure, and, as everyone knows, anyone who throws a monkey-wrench into that kind of machinery runs the risk of being described by its manipulators as a "citizen of the plain" if they ever get him down; but, exhausted and at the limit of his strength as Casement was, they were afraid of him.

He returned to England by way of the United States. Bryce, who was then our Ambassador there, came especially to New York to meet him and invited him to Washington. There he had conferences with members of the American Government and with President Taft. The result of this was encouraging, and Bryce reported to the Foreign Office that Casement roused a "personal interest in the matter among the higher authorities, which gives strong ground for believing that the publication of the report will be welcomed by the United States Government."

When Casement arrived in England with this backing, the British Government lost some of its inertia. Sir Edward Grey telegraphed to Washington that the report he had received from the British Minister in Lima was unsatisfactory. "The request for suggestions," he cabled, "cannot be regarded seriously as we have not ceased to make suggestions ever since the receipt of Sir Roger Casement's report, all of which have been disregarded. We feel that nothing will be done by the present Government, and that no progress will be made without publication of Sir Roger Casement's report."

The American Government approved the publication, and the press of the world was stirred to indignation by what the report revealed.

Casement was eulogized from the pulpit of Westminster Abbey in a sermon by Hensley Henson which was reported on the chief page of *The Times*. *The Times* also remarked in an editorial: "Sir Roger Casement has deserved well of his countrymen and of mankind by the ability and zeal with which he has investigated, under very difficult conditions, an appalling iniquity."

But if this report stirred the conscience of the world, it could only have been made by the lonely personal courage of the man who, surrounded by criminal greed in a murderous jungle, took his life in hand at every step. It was through publication of his report, and through this alone, that the evil system in the Putumayo was eventually destroyed and its leaders forced to take flight.

The effect on the British and American public for the time being was, for Roger Casement, that increase of justly earned prestige which, later on, Sir Basil Thomson and his colleagues thought it advisable to destroy in their carefully arranged campaign against his moral character. It was during this very time of selfless and high-minded achievement, in terrible strain, hardship and mortal peril, that, according to Sir Ernley Blackwell, Casement was leading a life of complete sexual self-indulgence.

In the meantime, referring to the exploitation of native populations in general, Casement wrote:

"It is atrocious—and I know, not from my heart alone but from my *head*, that it is true . . . between Leopoldism on the Congo, Diazism in Mexico, and what I know of the Amazon Rubber trade, there are more human beings held to-day in hopeless slavery, accompanied by the most inhuman cruelty, than at the height of the overseas slave trade. That is, I am convinced, a literal truth."

It was with these thoughts burning in his brain, overwrought by the emotional strain of all that he had been through, that Roger Casement returned to Ireland and what he believed to be the wrongs of his own countrymen.

CHAPTER VI

It is hardly surprising that under this long physical and emotional strain Sir Roger Casement's health broke down in 1913. He had achieved one of the greatest works of his generation for humanity; and he retired on that munificent pension of £421 a year with which F. E. Smith was to taunt him a few years later. The Irishman had "eaten the bread of England", said "Galloper" Smith. Casement at any rate believed that he was in the service of the "United Kingdom of Great Britain and Ireland" and in that capacity he was eating the bread of Ireland. Once in earlier days he had been the subject of a stupid and humourless reprimand by Whitehall for using some notepaper headed "Consulate of Great Britain and Ireland", and the bucket of cold water may have taught him that only complete submergence of his own nation would please the governing power.

Casement's retirement in Ireland on his meagre pension found him not resting, but quite selflessly working actively in the cause of Irish Nationalism. Slender as were his resources, he showed great generosity in his contributions to Irish schools. The following is an illustration both of this and of the spirit that had consistently animated him ever since his boyhood, as it had animated his father before him:

"I fear I could not give very much help because I have already promised over £100 this year to educational efforts in Ireland that are directed to a national end. These are a training college in Donegal, an Irish school in Galway, and a school in Dublin (St. Enda's) where the course of teaching is

Irish throughout, that is, a course designed primarily to interest boys in their own country and make them good and useful citizens of it. I was taught nothing about Ireland in Ballymena school—I don't think the word was ever mentioned in a single class of the school—and all I know of my country I learned outside the school. . . Patriotism has been stigmatized and often treated as 'treason' or as a 'crime', or dismissed with superior scorn as 'local' . . . As an Irishman I wish to see this state of things changed and Irish education to be primarily what that of every healthy people is—designed to build up a country from within, by training its youth to know, love and respect their own land before all other lands."

This passage may perhaps explain his proud bearing at the trial, when, as an Irishman, he openly admitted the charge of treason under English law.

Here in Ireland, Casement found that the Home Rule Bill, which had just been passed by the British Parliament, was threatened by Carson with arms imported from Germany. It was certainly not unnatural that the Nationalists of the South should think themselves entitled to take counter-measures. Was not the British Cabinet supporting Home Rule?

The spirit that was roused in him may be seen in the following extract from one of his letters:

"With the help of every drop of Fenian blood in my soul I hope it will light a fire that may set the Antrim hills ablaze. . . It is that sorry 'sympathy' for Ireland I mean to bury on the Antrim platform—and to unite (for I think it is possible) Presbyterian and Catholic farmers and townsmen at Ballymoney in a clear message to Ireland. . . It will mark the beginning of the uprising of the North.

"It will be a meeting, mind you, of *extraordinary* significance from the heart of Antrim, by Antrim men, Pres-
byterians and Protestants, and a flaming appeal to Ireland.
It will breathe much of the spirit of '98 and will be definitely
Irish—not of an English party at all. . .

"The Review [he had been present as a spectator at
Carson's parade of his Army] was good as a spectacle—but
Carson's face was awful. He looked 'the chief Traytour of
Ireland—a reprobate reserved for the sword'. I think the
man is very unhappy—he looked wretched, gloomy, dark
and foreboding, and the shadow of the Castle and its
'bloodhounds' was over him, and the greater gloom even of
the bloodshed yet to be. I am not against bloodshed in a
good cause but—for *this*."

Here is nothing small or mean. The tone is certainly on a
higher level than that of the men who declared that there
was *no* law they would not break.

And here comes an extraordinary complication: in spite
of the fact that Carson was in the opposite camp, Casement
took a strange pride in Carson's fighting qualities as an
Irishman. An amazing Irish tangle within the greater tangle
of loyalties, but not without its magnanimity. He would be
ready to see Ireland united, if united as a nation it could be,
under "King"[1] Carson, as the Ulster leader was now sometimes called:

"I feel I could not do anything else but go out and join
the 'grim, hard, determined Ulster face' when I see it being

---

[1] "A Belfast clergyman, inspecting a boys' school, asked: 'Can any of you
tell me who is the Supreme Being?' With one accord they cried 'Carson'—
all except one little lad who timidly suggested a more orthodox hypothesis.
'Ah, you Papist!' they shouted at the apostate." *Life of Lord Carson*, by Edward
Marjoribanks and Ian Colvin (1934).

shot at by Tommy Atkins. In fact, I'm absolutely certain I'd go! But I like Stacpoole's line of thought about Ireland and her spirit making one her children all. That's the right thought."

Later he wrote:

"And if I tell Irishmen their salvation cometh from the Liberals, I tell them what I don't believe—and what I do believe to be a lie. Civil war would be *far* better than to go on lying and pretending—if only we could be left free to fight out our battle here ourselves. . .

"Emigration will go up—it is rising even now—and no healthy thing will be done in all the land. The only healthy thing now is this Volunteer movement up here. It is fine; it is the act of men; and I like it, and love to think of those English Liberal Ministers squirming before those Ulster men who say: 'To hell with your politics—we mean to fight!' If only Ireland arose and said: 'I, too, mean to fight!— Then we might see daylight."

In contrast to the Northern Manifesto, appealing to the Kaiser for aid to crush the British Government, a Manifesto of the Irish Volunteers, drawn up by Casement, is less open to the charge of disloyalty, and the italicized passage, though more temperate in tone, is essentially at one with the statement by Sir Winston Churchill on page 33.

"*At a time when legislative proposals universally confessed to be of vital concern for the future of Ireland have been put forward, and are awaiting decision, a plan has been deliberately adopted by one of the great English political parties, advocated by the leaders of that party and by its numerous organs in the press, and brought systematically to bear on English public opinion, to make the display of military force and the menace of armed violence the determining*

68

factor in the future relations between this country and Great Britain.

"The party which has thus substituted open force for the semblance of civil government is seeking by this means not merely to decide an immediate political issue of grave concern to this Nation, but also to obtain for itself the future control of all our national affairs. It is plain to every man that the People of Ireland, if they acquiesce in this new policy by their inaction, will consent to the surrender, not only of their rights as a nation, but of their civil rights as men. . . If we fail to take such measures as will effectively defeat this policy, we become politically the most degraded population in Europe, and no longer worthy of the name of Nation. . . In a crisis of this kind the duty of safe-guarding our own rights is our first and foremost duty. . . From time immemorial it has been held by every race of mankind to be the right and duty of a freeman to defend his freedom with all his resources and with his life itself. The exercise of that right distinguishes the freeman from the serf, the discharge of that duty distinguishes him from the coward.

"To drill, to learn the use of arms, to acquire the habit of concerted and disciplined action, to form a citizen army from a population now at the mercy of almost any organized aggression—this, beyond all doubt, is a programme that appeals to all Ireland, but especially to young Ireland. . .

"The object proposed for the Irish Volunteers is to secure and maintain the rights and liberties common to all the people of Ireland. Their duties will be defensive and protective, and they will not contemplate either aggression or domination. Their ranks are open to all able-bodied Irishmen without distinction of creed, politics or social grade. . ."

There is irony in the fact that the "rebels" in the South

were in effect supporting the constitutional measure which the Unionists were threatening. In the face of such a situation it is not enough to use the glib adage "two wrongs do not make a right", when, as Casement himself observed in one of the noblest declarations of political faith ever made by an accused man, the greater treason led to the woolsack, while his own action led to the scaffold.

It soon became obvious to Casement that the Liberal Government would, in the face of Carson's army, abandon or dismember the Home Rule Bill. In another letter, telling his colleagues not to despair of getting arms to match those of the North (and if justice means anything to us, we must never lose sight of this, the key to the whole situation) he said:

"The game now, I see, is this. Under cover of 'an offer to Ulster' they are going to strip all the flesh off the Home Rule Bill—if we let them. Shall we? That is for you and others to think over. Meantime I am convinced the right and patriotic thing for all Irishmen to do is to go on with the Volunteers; volunteers in every county, city, town and village in Ireland. Don't despair of arms. I think we can get them. The Irish in America will not desert us in this crisis. I believe I can get you help from them the English little dream of to-day. . . The English are going to surrender to Carson.

"Don't despair, don't despond. We shall win, rest assured of that. Ireland was not born to suffering through the ages to end in death and despair at last. Her people have not kept their religion and their souls for nothing. . .

"This is the psychology of the situation. She (England) recoils from the Ulstermen, because they are not slaves—

and she knows it. They tell her to go to hell and propose to send her there, and you see, she draws back, talks of compromise, 'concession', while you and I, the mere Irish, are to take it in the old abject submission. Well, I for one won't—I mean to fight—and if John Bull betrays Ireland again, as I'm quite sure he means to do, then, with the help of God and *some* Irishmen, he'll learn that all Irishmen are not slaves and there is fight in us still."

From this point onwards, the events of his life moved with the inevitability of a Greek tragedy.

CHAPTER VII

ON THE 4TH of July, 1914, Casement went to America in the hope of raising funds from Irish-Americans for the Irish Volunteers. On July 26th in America he heard that Erskine Childers had successfully brought in 1,500 rifles to Howth, in Co. Dublin, and that the reaction of the British Liberal Government to this was remarkably different from its reaction to the 30,000 rifles brought into the North from Germany. A battalion of the King's Own Scottish Borderers was immediately despatched to Howth. They succeeded in shooting a certain number of civilians, but were beaten off by the Volunteers. It was thus upon the supporters of Home Rule that the first casualties were inflicted by the Liberal Government which had passed the measure The anger aroused in Southern Ireland and in Casement was a most natural consequence.

Against these killings a protest was organized in Philadelphia at which Casement was to be the chief speaker. However, on the day after the protest it was submerged by the outbreak of the First World War. But Casement had already taken the irrevocable step.

It is only with a clear remembrance of what had gone before, the anger aroused by the killing on the quays of Dublin, and the bland surrender by the Government to Carson, Smith and the gun-runners in the North, that Casement's next impulsive action can be justly weighed, but it was an action that burned his boats behind him. It had been rumoured that in addition to the surrender of the

Home Rule Bill, conscription was about to be enforced on the youth of Ireland. Rightly or wrongly, Casement believed this to be a betrayal of his countrymen, before whom Home Rule had been dangled and lawlessly snatched away. It must be remembered, too, that he was now surrounded by Irish-Americans who carried him along with them on a course where they themselves incurred no charge of treason. He wrote an open letter to the press. English readers may wince, as I do, at some of the things he says, but every chivalrous mind will recognize that his occasional injustices are the outcome of a justifiable indignation:

"New York, 17 September 1914.

"As an Irishman and one who has been identified with the Irish Volunteer movement since it began, I feel it my duty to protest against the claim now put forward by the British Government that, because that Government has agreed with its political opponents to 'place the Home Rule Bill on the Statute Book' and to defer its operation until after the war and until an 'Amending Bill' to profoundly modify its provisions has been introduced and passed, Irishmen in return should enlist in the British Army and aid the allied Asiatic and European powers in a war against a people who have never wronged Ireland. The British Liberal party has been publicly pledged for twenty-eight years to give self-government to Ireland. It has not yet fulfilled that pledge. Instead it now offers to sell, at a very high price, a wholly hypothetical and indefinite form of partial internal control of certain specified Irish services, if, in return for this promissory note (payable after death), the Irish people will contribute their blood, their honour and their manhood in a war that in no wise concerns them. Ireland has no quarrel with the German people or just cause of offence against them. . .

"Ireland has no blood to give to any land, to any cause but that of Ireland. Our duty as a Christian people is to abstain from bloodshed, and our duty as Irishmen is to give our lives for Ireland. Ireland needs all her sons. In the space of sixty-eight years her population has fallen by far over 4,000,000 souls, and in every particular of national life she shows a steady decline of vitality. Were the Home Rule Bill all that is claimed for it and were it freely given to-day, to come into operation to-morrow, instead of being offered for sale on terms of exchange that only a fool would accept, it would be the duty of Irishmen to save their strength and manhood for the trying tasks before them, to build up from a depleted population the fabric of a ruined national life.

"Ireland has suffered at the hands of British administrators a more prolonged series of evils, deliberately inflicted, than any other community of civilized men. To-day when no margin of vital strength remains for vital tasks at home, when its fertile fields are reduced by set design to producing animals and not men, the remnant of our people are being urged to lay down their lives on foreign fields, in order that the great and inordinately wealthy communities may grow greater and richer by the destruction of a rival's trade and industry. Had this war the highest moral aim in view, as its originators claim for it, it would still be the duty of Irishmen to keep out of it.

"If Irish blood is to be 'the seal that will bring all Ireland together in one nation and in liberties equal and common to all' then let that blood be shed in Ireland, where alone it can be righteously shed to secure those liberties. It was not Germany who destroyed the national liberties of the Irish people, and we cannot recover the national life struck down in our own land by carrying fire and sword into another land.

"The cause of Ireland is greater than the cause of any party; higher than the worth of any man; richer in its poverty than all the riches of Empire. If to-day we barter that cause in a sordid bargain, we shall prove ourselves unworthy of freedom—a dwindling race of cravens from whose veins the blood of manhood has been drained. If to now fight is our duty, then let us fight on that soil where so many generations of slain Irishmen lie in honour and fame. Let our graves be that patriot grass whence alone the corpse of Irish nationality can spring to life. Ireland will be 'false to her history, to every consideration of honour, good faith and self-interest' if she now willingly responds to the call of the British Government to send her brave sons and faithful hearts to fight in a cause that has no glint of chivalry or gleam of generosity in all its line of battle. If this be a war for the 'small nationalities', as its planners term it, then let it begin, for one small nationality, at home.

"Speaking as one of those who helped to found the Irish Volunteers, I say, in their name, that no Irishman fit to bear arms in the cause of his country's freedom can join the allied millions now attacking Germany in a war that at best concerns Ireland not at all and that can only add fresh burdens and establish a new drain, in the interest of another community, upon a people that has already been bled to the verge of Death.

"Roger Casement."

A psychologist would undoubtedly detect in this letter the overwrought emotion caused by what he had been through in his Putumayo investigations carried over into what he felt to be the wrongs of his own people.

The English reader with a short memory, if he thinks Casement's statement of Irish wrongs is exaggerated, will find a fully authenticated and documented statement of the plain facts in the article on Ireland in the Encyclopaedia Britannica (1911 edition), which has never been called a revolutionary textbook.

The common taunt that the Irish have never forgotten Cromwell loses its point in the record of outrage after outrage, culminating in what may be called the differential treatment of the gun-running at Larne in the North and that at Howth in the South.[1] In fairness we must put ourselves in Casement's position and realize the strength of his conviction that the first concern of Irishmen should be for their own country. There were aspects of the First World War which vitally concerned England, but it is useless at this time of day to pretend that these aspects were not overlaid with falsehood by the machinery of propaganda. The mind that could apprehend all the real truth behind the propaganda had to be of a very complex order; and Casement, while he was too honest to be misled by the superficial slogans of the hour, was too single-minded to see anything but the cause to which he had devoted himself. Rightly or wrongly he felt with passion that an Ireland whose population had been decimated by oppression should not be conscripted into war for a cause which he felt was not her own, since England, as he sincerely thought, had at that very

[1] See Appendix I.

76

moment surrendered the cause of Home Rule to the armed threats of its opponents.

Casement did not regard the Irish problem as one that concerned only the United Kingdom. For him it was a part of the general cause of humanity, and he asserted its right to be treated on an international level. In this he was simply expressing a view which Gladstone expressed, in his famous speech on Home Rule.

"It has now," said Gladstone, *"become a question in the strictest sense between a nation and a nation, and not only between a nation and a nation, but between a great nation and a small nation, between a strong nation and a weak nation, between a wealthy nation and a poor nation."*

Rightly or wrongly, Casement thought himself better entitled to talk with the representatives of foreign powers than were Carson or F. E. Smith. Whether this was pride or vanity (or what, in the seats of the mighty at Scotland Yard, was called idealistic megalomania), it was not personal or selfish.

But now that the First World War had broken out, he could hardly have expected anything more than the icily regular tone of the letter from Arthur Nicholson, British Permanent Under-Secretary of State:

"Sir:
"The attention of the Secretary of State has been called to a letter, dated New York, September 17th, which appeared in the *Irish Independent* of 5th October over your signature. The letter urges that Irish sympathies should be with Germany rather than with Great Britain and that Irishmen should not join the British Army. As you are still liable,

77

under certain circumstances, to be called to serve under the Crown, I am to request you to state whether you are the author of the letter in question.

"I am, Sir,

"Your most obedient, humble servant."

It was quite clear that there could be no reconciliation between Casement's kind of nationalism and the kind of British patriotism which Englishmen, by an oddly Hibernian paradox, thought was their due from the Irishmen whom they had just been killing.

After consultation with his Irish-American colleagues, Casement was at once drawn into the plans of John Devoy, the Irish-American leader, who, with John Redmond's speech in Chicago to encourage him, had already gone much further than Casement probably realized at this time. The powerful group of Irish-Americans had already envisaged that organized rebellion which was to culminate in the "Easter Rising". This Rising a little later, and when it was too late, Casement, and Casement alone among the founders of the Irish Volunteers, strove desperately to avert. This will appear very clearly on a later page. Devoy and his friends had already anticipated a manifesto from the Kaiser, promising freedom and independence to Ireland, and Casement, swept off his feet by the unprecedented happenings in Ireland, was introduced by Devoy to the German Ambassador in Washington, von Bernstorff, who for obvious reasons feigned a sympathy for the Irish cause which he did not feel, and held out false hopes and promises.

After consultations with his Irish-American colleagues it was decided that Casement should make his way to Germany via Norway, and obtain the pledge from the German Government that in the event of their victory they would guarantee the freedom and independence of Ireland.

This, whether it were treason or not, and whether it gives a fair picture or not, was how it appeared to an impulsive Irishman; and to any fair-minded Englishman, however insular, it should at least be comprehensible. In the circumstances it was the kind of thing that our own Raleigh might have done. Carson had been prepared to take the responsibility for civil war with German aid, and Casement felt justified in trying to obtain that pledge.

He obtained it, but it was worthless. In his overwrought state he plunged headlong into the impossible scheme of a quixotic dreamer, and into a misguided action from which the leaders on the other side drew back only just in time to save themselves from the charge of treason in the most formidable sense.

It is only right to recognize that this sensitive and impetuous man, who all his life had been fighting against official red tape, fighting a lonely battle on behalf of the oppressed, with whom he numbered his Irish compatriots, did not look upon his cause as subordinate to any other, and he might feel as fully entitled as his opponents to independent action.

Count Bernstorff gave Casement an introduction to the German Minister in Norway, and paved the way for his journey to Berlin.

This, of course, was more than an irrevocable step. In an Englishman it would have been treason—but hardly in an Irish Nationalist, in the unprecedented circumstances. Even in an Irish Nationalist, however, with that burning faith in his cause which Casement undoubtedly had, his action was

79

now at least a fatal blunder. He was exchanging the devil he knew for one he did not know. He was soon to realize that, whatever the faults of the British Government Departments might be, the faults of the German Government Departments were far worse and far more exasperating.

CHAPTER VIII

On the eve of Casement's departure for Germany, via Norway, a young Norwegian, Adler Christensen, was engaged by him as a servant. The accounts of how he met Christensen differ in phraseology, according to the presence or absence of the narrator's desire to suggest that the association was scandalous. One thing is quite certain: the derogatory phrases, so far as Casement is concerned, have not the slightest evidence to support them. And it was Casement's good qualities that made the attack possible.

In the genuine diary which Casement kept while in Germany and which was later published in Munich, Casement tells how he was stopped by a young Norwegian sailor on Broadway, who asked for help on the ground that he was unemployed and starving. He spun a pitiful tale about ill-treatment, but "he was grateful for my help and I saw him once or twice in New York, where with the help I gave him he got work."

Casement was aware that he was being watched, but does not seem to have suspected Christensen, whom three months later he took into his personal employment to accompany him on his journey via Norway to Berlin. He writes:

"As a double precaution I engaged a man, whom I had already helped when in difficulties and who was grateful for this help, to carry the few papers I thought it essential to bring with me. This man, by name Adler Christensen, was a native of Norway, had been for some years a sailor—and latterly at work in America. He booked his passage in second

81

class to return to Norway to visit his parents at Moss."

The purpose is quite clear, as a Norwegian on this voyage could be of great use. But after forty years of doctoring and passing from mouth to mouth, this is how the story has been received by Mr. René MacColl. The starvation, it will be noted, has receded into the background and something else has taken its place:

"On a stroll down Broadway that evening he picked up a young Norwegian sailor named Adler Christensen. This unlikely character attached himself to Casement. . . . Christensen was a plump twenty-four year old who had expensive tastes and used make-up."

The something else that has been substituted for starvation is the word "plump", and the reference to cosmetics, and though the latter has been mentioned by many scandal-mongers, they have seldom had the courage to quote the passage from one of Casement's letters which is the only basis for their misleading statement.

The editor of the Munich diary gives a facsimile letter from Sir Roger Casement to Christensen, expressing his disgust at a certain change in Christensen's habits after he had become better off and fallen into bad ways in Berlin. In remonstrance Casement uses the phrase: "My dear faithful old Adler", for Casement, all too simply perhaps, believed that Christensen had saved him from a plot against his life in Christiania. He continues: "you buy things you don't need at all, like that raincoat and the gloves, etc. I have *no* gloves, and you have about 6 pairs!—and face and complexion 'blooms' and God knows what. All you need is some healthy work to keep your mind occupied."

It is unfortunate that Mr. René MacColl in quoting this

passage omits the contemptuous phrase "and God knows what", also the passage about healthy good work. In an earlier passage in his Munich diary Casement had noticed with some uneasiness a change in Christensen's manner: "He no longer looks me in the face." But Casement still believed that Christensen earlier had given him a true account of the plot in Christiania.

A few hours after their arrival there Christensen said that the British Minister Findlay had offered him £5,000 to kidnap his employer or get him knocked on the head. It was an amazing story, and it has certain flaws which John Buchan would hardly have allowed in a work of fiction. But Casement, in what Conrad called the limpidity of his character, swallowed the story whole. He was convinced that Christensen had been most faithfully proof against the bribe to betray his master. After stating in his Munich diary that the ship arrived in Christiania on October 29th, 1914, he says:

"We had stopped at Christiansand that morning . . . whence my man, Adler Christensen, had sent a telegram to his father at Moss saying that he hoped to arrive home (after 12 years' absence) on the following Friday, 31 October.

"I went on shore about 1.30 a.m. and drove to the Grand Hotel. . .

"Alder went down to breakfast about 9 with instructions to 'walk about' and keep his eyes open. He returned to me about 11.45 a.m. in a state of great excitement, and threw down some Norwegian paper money (25 Kronen in notes) saying he had just come from the British Legation, where the Minister himself had given him these notes and had made certain proposals to him about me that were, as I said when he told me, 'absolutely incredible'. There was, however, no doubt of the sincerity of my man or of his anger and resentment. . . .

"The story, in brief, was this. When Adler had had his breakfast . . . he had been in the large hall of the hotel when a stranger brushed up against him and said 'Go to the telephone booth and call up No. 11460 and you will hear something good.' . . . He then called up the number given and was told in answer: 'Take a taxi-cab and come up to 79 Drammensveien.'

"Here he found a gentleman 'a very tall man, clean shaven except for a short greyish moustache, with his hair brushed straight back, and dressed in a tweed suit'. This gentleman at once began proceedings by announcing 'I am the British Minister' and locking the door. He instantly plunged *in medias res*, and unfolded his intentions towards myself with a boldness that, as Adler said, quite won his admiration—but not his sympathy. He began by telling my man he knew all about him and me—'You are Adler Christensen, from Moss, and you sent a telegram from Christiansand to your father, and yesterday you sent a cablegram from your friend Mr. James. . . . to New York —now I want the original of that cablegram to have his handwriting.' He went on to say that he knew all about me; that I was 'Sir Roger' and that I was going to Germany, he was sure, to conspire with the Germans about Ireland. He said the Irish had rebelled before but 'did he tell you they ever succeeded?' 'They will not succeed this time either.' 'He is going to be fooled by the Germans; they don't care anything about Ireland and only want to make trouble for

England.' This and more, in an extreme frankness and bold-ness.

"Adler made no protest when my right name was men-tioned and as the Minister proceeded he appeared to be influenced by his argument and to sympathize with the Minister's point of view as between England and Germany. After this dissertation on the state of Ireland, past and present, Mr. Findlay came to the point, on the clear assump-tion that the man before him was a mercenary ruffian who would carry out his wishes for a suitable reward. He said he wished greatly to stop my getting to Germany and suggested it might be managed.

"Adler said I had been 'very good' to him and had 'befriended him when in trouble' and that I 'trusted him implicitly'. Mr. Findlay met this by pointing out that I was entirely defenceless in Norway, with no friends to appeal to and no government to raise enquiry if I 'disappeared'. 'He cannot claim to be Mr. James . . ., because his papers are false and the true Mr. . . . is in New York. The American Legation cannot intervene because he doesn't belong to them; the German Minister dare not; and we should protect and help whoever got him for us.' He then suggested my being made away with in a full-blooded hint on which point Adler Christensen is quite clear.—The Minister did not say to Adler 'you do it'—but suggested what he wanted thus: He said 'I suppose you would not mind having an easy time all the rest of your life, with nothing to do? Well, now, this man could be got out of the way, and no one will know.' 'If someone knocked him on the head he would get well paid for it.'

"Adler protested that whoever did that would get into

85

trouble and pay the penalty—but Mr. Findlay pointed out that there could be no enquiry, as 'no one would disappear'. Sir Roger was not in Norway—and Mr. James . . . was in New York.

"He went on to say that anything done to me would be very well paid for indeed—and that I might be 'got hold of' and handed over to the British Government.

"He terminated the interview, of which the foregoing is only a compressed synopsis, by giving Adler 25 Kronen in notes 'for your taxi-cab fares' and telling him to think it all over and 'if you agree, to come here at three o'clock this afternoon.'

"I determined that my man should return at three o'clock. . . . The interview that followed was a lengthy one for it was nearly five o'clock when Adler returned . . . and handed me a hundred Kronen Norwegian note, the first proceeds of his new role of assassin extraordinary to the British Envoy Extraordinary. . . . Adler said he showed plainly he was a blackguard and took the Minister at the same valuation. . . The understanding arrived at was that Adler was to remain in my service and do his best to get me decoyed to . . where I might be captured by British men of war, . . . and as much proof as possible against me and my Irish associates. For this service, Mr. Findlay guaranteed to Adler 'on my honour', the sum of £5,000 sterling. . . ."

Casement accepted the story simply. His overwrought mental condition and the sincerity of his belief that a plot had been laid against his life is again apparent in his feverish anxiety to obtain evidence against Findlay; and when he arrived in Berlin he sent Christensen back to Christiania in an attempt to interview Findlay and collect more evidence.

He was then troubled in conscience by something which would never have occurred to his caluminators. He wrote in his diary:

"I waited in some anxiety, I must admit. I was exposing this young man, whose life since he was a little boy of 12 had been one of great hardship, to a very great temptation."

Later he wrote to Christensen:

"I want you to become an honest good man, dear Adler, and to help you to this—and so I am really unhappy when I think of you telling lies for me."

There is some excuse for Casement's acceptance of Christensen's story, with all its embroideries, for Christensen undoubtedly obtained, in Findlay's writing, a guarantee of £5,000 for information which would lead to the capture of his employer (a facsimile of this guarantee is given in the Munich diary). Capture, of course, is a very different thing from assassination, and the offer of this reward in wartime in no way impugned the honour of the British Minister.

At a later date reports reached Casement about Christensen's behaviour in Berlin. Under questioning by Casement, Christensen made a confession which obviously distressed his employer. The entry in his Munich diary under December 18th, 1914, is exactly the opposite of what has been insinuated; in fact it might have been written by any good Army Chaplain:

"*I feel it would be far safer for all concerned to send Adler back to Norway and let him return to U.S.A. to work there. I told him much of this last night—and said I would try to get him good work there, if he would promise to go straight and quite give up doing the things he confessed to me the last night before he returned to Moss he had done.*"

87

Mr. MacColl's remark that in what he calls "the Christensen affair" Casement was "*vaunting* a *secret* passion" is quite incompatible with the whole tone of Casement's own words, which are those of a kindly master to a faithful servant.

What is the explanation of the extraordinary difference between the contents of the black diaries, which are supposed to have recorded those daily unnatural offences, and the cleanness of the Munich diary and what he says about Christensen? Are we to suppose that Casement's friends forged a clean diary, clean letters and a clean moral character to cover the very period in which, according to Sir Ernley Blackwell, he was in a state of moral degradation?

The Munich diary is that of a man who, whatever his political blunders may have been, was in character exactly the opposite of the poor creature depicted in the spurious diary, with suspiciously perfect timing, by the men who had a clear motive for blackening it behind the scenes of the trial.

But we can go much further than this: How are we to account for the fact that in all the voluminous writings of Sir Roger Casement there is no trace of the propensities attributed to him *except* in the documents which passed through the hands of Sir Basil Thomson, and which historians are not allowed to examine for authentication?

The simple quixotry of Casement's character was so incomprehensible to the German authorities that many of them suspected him to be a peculiarly crafty English agent. As a guarantee of his sincerity he proposed the formation of an Irish Brigade from the Irish prisoners of war. They were to be given an Irish uniform and an emerald flag of their own. Here indeed was that tilting at windmills which the children of this world have agreed to regard as at least not altogether worldly or dishonourable. He was involved in impossible contradictions in the "treaty" which he drew up with the Germans, stipulating that in no circumstances should this Brigade be used for German purposes or against England, but only—on repatriation—as a contingent of the Irish Volunteers.

The Germans naturally tried to stretch the limits imposed on them by this "treaty"; and here again, taking advantage of his known feeling for the small nationalities, they may have induced him to say something rash about the use of the Irish Brigade to fight for Egypt against the Turks. This was alleged against him later, as a justification for his execution, but the "treaty", futile as it was, expressly deprived the Germans of the right to give any such orders.

From a German point of view this was fantastically naïve, and they regarded him as a dangerous visionary. The only use they could make of him was to get him back to Ireland as quickly as possible in the hope that he would be a source of trouble there to England instead of to themselves.

Casement's plan, almost pathetic in its futility, was the chief charge against him at his trial. It was said that he had seduced fifty Irish prisoners of war from their allegiance to England; but what of those Englishmen who had induced a mutiny in the British army at the Curragh, wherein British officers, rightly or wrongly, rendered themselves liable to court-martial?

If Casement was a "selfless idealist", as he was constantly called, not only by his friends, but in derision by his enemies, it was at least unwise to hang him.

He soon began to realize that the Germans had no sympathy whatever with selfless ideals, and he felt that he had walked into a cage from which there was no exit but one.

And here came the bleakest of all the ironies that bedevilled and befooled this lonely adventurer on his quest for something that could not be found.

He was like a man who, in estrangement from one set of acquaintances, had turned to strangers for friendship, and found them even colder, more brutal and more materialistic than the others. There was a kind of naïveté in his assumption that the unknown must be better than the known. He now found it far worse.

News reached him from America that plans had been made for an Easter Rising in Ireland, and he realized now in something like panic that it would lead to quite futile shedding of blood. He spoke of this to the German Foreign Office and Admiralty, and saw only cold derision in their eyes. He tried to send a message to the Irish Volunteers in the hope of averting the disaster, and was threatened by the Germans with denunciation to his Irish-American friends as a betrayer of their cause. Below are extracts from his Berlin diary, now in the National Library of Ireland in Dublin.

April 2nd, 1916: "I am already a dead man, but not yet a wholly dishonoured one, despite all my mistakes. God knows they were not for self."

"I go on because I am fool enough, or brave enough, or coward enough. . . I feel like a man already damned. . . I feel that all is indeed lost, and the sooner my life is taken from me the better."

He tried to outwit the Germans by inducing them to send him to Ireland in a submarine, ostensibly to help in the

Rising, but actually in the hope of arriving in time to prevent it. Franz H. J. Zerhusen had been appointed Liaison Officer with the Irish Brigade in Germany, perhaps because he had been a member of the Gaelic League and some ten years earlier had married an Irish girl. He seems to have understood what Casement had in mind. Much of Zerhusen's statement is confused, but three facts stand out clearly:

(i) That Casement, when arrangements were being made for him to go to Ireland, had refused to take a contingent of the Irish Brigade with him because he thought it would be throwing their lives away;

(ii) That there was an angry scene at the German Foreign Office about this, at which he was present with Robert Monteith, a special representative of the Irish Republican Army and of the Irish-American leaders;

(iii) That Casement, on the eve of his departure with Monteith and Bailey, was sure that he was going to his own death, and had said to Zerhusen: "The sad part of this is that nobody will ever know why we go to Ireland."

Eventually, and too late, the Germans granted his request that he be sent in a submarine, ahead of the ship containing the arms. (These afterwards turned out to be outworn and useless weapons captured from the Russians.) Even here there are some grounds for suspecting that arrangements had been made for his own capture and that he instinctively knew it. When asked by the German captain of the submarine if he needed any additional clothes before landing, he replied "Only my shroud."

A delay was caused by the breaking down of the submarine in which he had embarked, and the necessity of transferring him to another.

His knowledge that he was going to his death gives poignancy to his own description of what he felt as he touched Irish earth again:

"When I landed in Ireland that morning (about 3 a.m.) swamped and swimming ashore on an unknown strand, I was happy for the first time for over a year. Although I knew that this fate waited on me, I was for one brief spell happy and smiling once more. I cannot tell you what I felt. The sand-hills were full of skylarks, rising in the dawn, the first I had heard for years—the first sound I heard through the surf was their song as I waded in through the breakers, and they kept rising all the time up to the old rath at Currshone, where I stayed and sent the others on, and all around were primroses and wild violets and the singing of the skylarks in the air, and I was back in Ireland again. As the day grew brighter I was quite happy, for I felt all the time it was God's will that I was there. The only person alive—if he be alive— who knows the whole story of my coming, and why I came, with what aim and hope, is Monteith. I hope he is alive and that you may see him and he will tell you everything, and then you will know that the very thing I am blamed for, and am dying for, was quite what you would have wished me to do. It is a cruel thing to die with all men misunder-standing—misapprehending—and to be silent for ever."[1]

[1] From a private letter to his sister, Mrs. Nina Newman, written in the condemned cell in Pentonville Gaol July 25th, 1916.

CHAPTER IX

THE ARREST of Casement in a ruined fort near the coast shortly after he landed has been described so often that the details need not be repeated here. We must now consider the dilemma presented to the British Government in view of Casement's high reputation.

The Cabinet was afraid that Casement might be canonized as a martyred patriot in Ireland and in America; and exactly at this crucial moment F. E. Smith laid before them something which might solve this very difficulty. A coincidence most remarkable! It was alleged to have been discovered by Basil Thomson. He reported (and the several reports which he afterwards published were all contradictory of one another) that an obscene diary (singular) had been found among Casement's effects. How far the Attorney-General was able to provide Thomson with material from the archives[1] may be a matter of conjecture, but F. E. Smith's motive—the destruction of the movement against which he had been prepared to wage civil war—certainly explained his eagerness for the use of the diary, and his attempt to impose (as will be seen later) quite untrue accounts of the time and place of its discovery both upon the Court and upon the readers of his book *Famous Trials*.

To smear the leader would carry with it the advantage of sullying the Irish movement, of which Casement's accusers

[1] For a view of Smith's unscrupulousness over government archives, even after he had ceased to be Attorney-General, see memoirs of his successor, Sir Patrick Hastings.

were the most implacable enemies. On the remarkable advice of the legal representative of the Home Office, Sir Ernley Blackwell, officially typed copies of the diary were "by judicious means" circulated behind the scenes to influence public opinion. His Memorandum to the Cabinet, as quoted in my first chapter from *Hansard* of May 3rd, 1956, reads:

"So far as I can judge, it would be far wiser from every point of view to allow the law to take its course and by judicious means to use these diaries [plural] to prevent Casement attaining martyrdom."

A feeble defence of this wicked suggestion is the statement that Sir Ernley Blackwell intended them to be used only after the execution of Casement, but the fact remains that officially typed copies were privately shown to influential persons who would otherwise have signed a petition for reprieve. Here again a feeble defence has been made that "this was the work of underlings". But a typed copy was imposed upon King George V. He in turn showed it to Hensley Henson, the Anglican dignitary who, consistently with his praise of Casement in Westminster Abbey, would otherwise have signed the petition. Evidence of this is in a letter from Dean Inge who, never dreaming that the Sovereign himself could be thus imposed upon, naïvely took that fact as proof of the authenticity of the infamous document. On December 24th, 1953, he wrote to me: "I feel sure that Casement was a man of infamous character. The King showed my friend Hensley Henson the diary, which of course the Irish say was forged."

The imposition of this document upon the Sovereign was one of the gravest features of the whole affair, since the King had been doing his utmost to reconcile the conflicting elements in Ireland.

No diary was offered at the trial, although a typed copy was offered to the defence with a still more remarkable suggestion that if they cared to accept it as true and plead insanity, the prosecution, which later was to agree with Blackwell that Casement was not insane, would nevertheless co-operate with the defence to brand him with the moral stigma and have him incarcerated in a lunatic asylum. This of course would have been all that was necessary to prevent any acclaim of a patriot martyr. However, the generous offer was refused.

Petitions for a reprieve were prepared and were signed by many men and women of the highest integrity. One of the most ardent appeals for a reprieve was made by Sir Cecil Spring-Rice, who was not only one of the best Ambassadors we have ever had in Washington, but the author of those lines so frequently sung in Westminster Abbey, expressing that love for England,

> The love that asks no question,
> The love that pays the price,
> The love that makes undaunted
> The final sacrifice.

It was known that the American Senate was about to support the appeal for reprieve and there was little question that it would have succeeded but for the intensive campaign in which the alleged diary was circulated, "by judicious means" and (as will be shown) without the knowledge of the victim.

It will be well here to examine the remarkably contradictory reports of the "discovery". There are four accounts, and the contradictions are so glaring and so obviously motivated that in a Court of law under cross-examination Basil Thomson would have been convicted of deliberate perjury.

Two trunks, which Casement had left in his old lodgings in Ebury Street more than two years previously, had been brought to Scotland Yard just over a year and a quarter before his interrogation there; but if the world was to be convinced that there had been no tampering with the alleged diary "discovered" therein, there was an obvious advantage, from Basil Thomson's point of view, in his lie about the date and manner of discovery. The reader will bear in mind that the "locked trunks" had been at Scotland Yard at least sixteen months at the time of the interview with Casement, but Basil Thomson, clearly for the purpose mentioned above, deliberately stated that they had been brought "locked" from Ebury Street during the actual course of the interview. In an article in *The Times* of November 21st, 1921, he said:

"Towards the end of the interview *a policeman who had been sent to search Casement's old lodgings in London, entered the room and said that he had brought away two or three trunks of clothing and wanted the key to unlock them. . . I asked Casement for the key and with a magnificent gesture he said: 'Break them open. There is nothing in them but clothing and I don't want the trunks again.' There was something in them besides clothing—a diary with occasional gaps from the year 1903.*"

In this statement, coming from the head of the C.I.D., it is impossible for the falsity to be accidental. A year and four months is not a minor discrepancy.

One must picture the scene: standing there, still wearing the drenched clothes in which he had been tumbled out of the canvas boat into the sea at Tralee Bay, Casement, whose pockets had been searched four times by the police and the contents (with no keys among them) officially noted and appropriated by the police, is asked by the head of the C.I.D. (so Sir Basil Thomson says) to produce at a moment's notice from those *empty* pockets the key (in the singular) of the trunks (in the plural) which had been abandoned two years before in London.

The picture is as preposterous in its minor details as in its major and demonstrable falsehood. We are asked to believe that when Scotland Yard had been collecting all the evidence it could find against Casement and had actually had these trunks in its possession for a year and four months, in wartime, it was so constrained by delicacy of feeling that it refrained from examining them until the very moment when it suited Sir Basil to be surprised by the discovery of a diary. And that key which Sir Basil mentions several times in the singular to locked trunks in the plural? Well, of course there was only one diary and Sir Basil knew where it was. He could no more have expected his words to be subjected to analysis than he could have expected two keys to be found in the empty pockets of that man cast up by the sea. (Defoe said that Robinson Crusoe, having taken all his clothes off on the beach, swam out to a wreck and filled his pockets with ship's biscuits! But that was in an avowed work of fiction.) Naturally, to a mind on only one certain trunk there would be need for one key only—but it was a revealing slip.

Perhaps realizing the unlikelihood of this story, he wrote another version in his book *Queer People* (1922):

"*Some months earlier*, when we first had evidence of Casement's treachery, his London lodgings had been visited and his locked trunks removed to Scotland Yard. Towards the end of the interview a policeman entered the room and whispered to me that Casement might have the key to the trunks. I asked him, and with a magnificent gesture he said 'Break them open; there is nothing in them but clothing and I shall not want them again.' But something beside clothing was found in one of the trunks—a diary and a cash book from the year 1903, with considerable gaps."

He undoubtedly made the alterations with the first version before him, because he repeats certain clauses word for word, and with meticulous accuracy. If the documents were really genuine, would he have resorted to this deception?

The alterations have been defended on the unconsciously comic ground that the head of the C.I.D. was not meticulously accurate (in matters of life and death?). But why is he so meticulously accurate in clauses where no purpose could be served by any alteration, and so very meticulously inaccurate in just those clauses where an obvious purpose is served by a falsehood? There is a touch of ironic comedy in the fact that when Thomson was arrested at a later date for an offence in Hyde Park his excuse was that he was "collecting evidence".

The motives for the alterations are, however, plain. Since the trunks had really been brought to Scotland Yard sixteen months before the interrogation, he could hardly expect that his first statement would stand up to closer scrutiny. But he still minimized the time as far as was in his power; he still maintained that the trunks had not been opened until the policeman asked him to get the key (in the singular) out of Casement's empty pockets. The policeman apparently knew before the trunks were opened that they contained clothes; and it will be noted that a cash book has been added, and that the gaps in the diary have become "considerable" and not "occasional" (later on, the find developed into five diaries and three ledgers, all containing indecent matter).

A third version appeared in 1925 (*English Life*, March issue). By this time Thomson had perhaps realized the further unlikelihood, when Scotland Yard had been combing the world for evidence against Casement, of the trunks having been left unexamined for so long. In this new version the detective entered while Casement was being examined by Thomson and informed him in a whisper that some months earlier Casement's landlord had brought two trunks to Scotland Yard. Had Sir Roger the *keys*? The discovery was again made of "a diary and a cashbook" but Thomson still carefully refrains from saying that the trunks had been there sixteen months—for of course we must not allow too much time for the forgery. He is obliged to allow more than he did earlier, but it is still a minimum.

In his fourth account (*The Scene Changes*, published in 1939) Basil Thomson had evidently realized that the story of the "locked trunks" and the "key" or "keys" will not wash, and he gives us yet another version, adroitly shifting the responsibility to the Superintendent of the Special Branch and the location to Casement's luggage:

"Our interview was but half completed when Patrick Quinn, Superintendent of the Special Branch, peered round the door with the expression of Mephistopheles, tiptoed up to my table and deposited a MS. volume upon it. He then withdrew discreetly and left the

interview to proceed. Whether Casement recognized the volume [in the singular] *or not I am unable to say. At any rate it did not appear to confuse him. Quinn had abstracted it from his luggage, which was lying in the Special Branch office. It was a diary, and when I came to examine it after the interview I realized that it could not be printed in any language."*

There is, however, good evidence that to a chosen few the spurious diary had actually been exhibited in 1915. Casement's cousin Mrs. Sidney Parry, the meticulous honesty of whose statements has never been questioned and is indeed borne out by her abstention from affirming anything of which she was not absolutely sure, has placed on record in the National Library in Dublin a statement of which an excerpt is given below. Her account of the finding of the trunks in Ebury Street is factual and complete, in sharp distinction from all the varied official accounts:

"As a matter of fact, the trunks left behind by Roger in Ebury St. were handed over to the police by the landlady, at the instigation of another lodger, as soon as Roger went to Germany in 1914. Sir B.T. had the diary in his possession at least 16 months before Roger's trial, and he had plenty of time to see that it was so doctored as to suit his purpose long before the time he needed it for propaganda purposes. It was shown to various people sometime during 1915, I think at the end of 1915 but am not sure."

The writer of this letter who, with her friend Mrs. John Richard Green, worked unremittingly for the reprieve, was a woman of the most honourable character, and not only a near relative but an intimate friend of Casement. Professor J. H. Morgan's tribute to her is given in the last chapter of this book.

Her statement that the diary was being shown in 1915 completely contradicts all four conflicting accounts by Basil Thomson, as well as that of F. E. Smith. In this connection it should be noted that the well-known New York lawyer, John Quinn, legal representative of the Standard Oil Company, left definite testimony that he believed the British had the diary before 1916. He may have heard this from his friend Spring-Rice, for, after the execution of Casement, when news of the diary was being spread by British officials, Quinn wrote to Spring-Rice and referred to the fact that the British had the diaries while Casement was in Germany but used them officially only when he was powerless to reply.

A curious thing about all these accounts is that there is not the slightest suggestion of the "five immense volumes and three ledgers" into which, as will be seen, the story later developed. Perhaps the interpolations had not yet been completed. Sufficient for the day was the evil thereof; after all, a work of art takes time. Possibly it had not yet dawned upon the artist or artists that there would later be very strong pressure for authentication, but if the advice of Sir Ernley Blackwell to a "wavering Cabinet" were to be followed, and the smearing documents "by judicious means" shown to heads of Governments who might ask for authentication, the work would have to be expertly and strongly supported.

Although Casement was being questioned at great length it will be noticed that Thomson did not ask him a single question about the MS. volume which he says was so impressively laid before him. There is no indication that he even looked at it until the examination was over, although the interruptions, theatrical exits and entrances of the police, the request for the keys, and final production of the object from the locked trunks, would surely have provoked some slight question, even if only: "What is this?" There was a stenographer present, and if a question had been asked Casement's reply might have been disconcerting, and of course the stenographer would have noted it. One can hardly wonder that Thomson's statements about the book were officially declared to be unauthorized.

If the interpolations were to be successful, something authentic in Casement's handwriting, with dates and places, would have to be found. It is again a most remarkable coincidence that the diary found in 1916 is for the year 1903 (Basil Thomson says *from* 1903—in itself an unusual phrase for a single diary) and this is exactly the year for which there would have been accessible in the Government archives the reports in Casement's own handwriting with dates and places of his investigations in the Congo. Still more remarkable is the coincidence that the only other section of the diary of which typed copies have been shown (as lately as 1956) is for the years 1910 and 1911, for which again there were in accessible archives the reports, with dates and places in Casement's own writing, of the Putumayo investigation, together with the diary, or extracts from the diary, of Armando Normand.

If the matter had been left there, the "considerable gaps" might at least have aroused suspicion, so perhaps we have here an explanation of why a single volume gradually developed into five, of whose discovery there is no record at all.

The suggestion that the labour of making the interpolations would have been too great hardly bears examination in view of what was done in a more legitimate way to deceive the enemy. The case of *Operation Heartbreak*, about which Lord Norwich (Mr. Duff-Cooper) and Mr. Ewan Montague each wrote an entire volume, is an example of the way in which, once a game of this kind is begun, the participants become more and more interested in its successful completion down to the last detail. Interest is naturally heightened if the consequences of detection are likely to be serious.

The object which at the time seemed important to the manipulators of propaganda was as far as possible to alienate sympathy from the movement with which Casement was associated, especially among the Irish-Americans who were supporting him financially as well as politically. This is the only explanation of the unprecedented scale on which the smear campaign was conducted.

There is clear evidence that, with perfect timing, the groundwork had been prepared *before* Sir Basil Thomson's "discovery". On April 15th, 1916, exactly a week earlier, the *Daily Chronicle* published a *Reuter* report from Copenhagen that the *Kolding Avis* (a little known journal at the other end of Denmark, most conveniently remote from London) had stated that Casement had been arrested (in Germany) on an unspecified charge. The *Daily Mail*, on April 26th, 1916, stated:

"Simultaneously with the issue of this message, a mysterious report was circulated in London, alleging that Casement had been arrested for an offence under Paragraph 175 of the German Code", i.e., the paragraph dealing with unnatural vices. This, of course, was also untrue, an anticipation by some only too eager soul brooding hopefully on things to come.

Incidentally, the Danish newspaper had actually said that Casement had been arrested for swindling, and this, by two successive stages, as in the parlour game called "Scandal", became first an unspecified charge, then a charge only too clearly specified, all three of them being absolutely untrue.

It is plain from the foregoing that both before the "discovery" and after the instructions to stop (*v.* page 107) the calumny was at work. It was useful preparation for the way of the Attorney-General.

The only other account of the discovery may be traced to the most amazing falsification of all: F. E. Smith, in his book *Famous Trials* (Hutchinson & Co.), giving his own account of the case in which, as Attorney-General, he appointed himself Prosecutor, calmly states:

". . In 1916, on Good Friday . . persons in Tralee saw a light at sea, and during the night a boat came to the shore containing three men. One was Casement, another was Bailey, a member of the Irish Brigade who had joined with a view to getting back home if he could. When they landed the boat was abandoned on the beach, and Bailey buried there some maps of Ireland of foreign origin, and three coats, *one of which contained Casement's diary.*"

It was after the publication of this statement that Sir Basil Thomson amended his three earlier contradictory stories and said that the diary had been found "in Casement's luggage", a word that might be regarded as bridging the gap between the locked trunks in Ebury Street and what Casement had brought with him from Germany (*v.* page 126).

As for the photostatic extracts, there is good evidence to the fact that in the Putumayo report Casement included a translation, in his own handwriting, of the Armando Normand diary.

Mr. Bulmer Hobson, late permanent official of the Revenue Department, Dublin, has placed on record in the National Library of Ireland this statement:

"When Roger Casement returned to Ireland after his investigation of the conditions in the Putumayo I saw him almost daily, and we had many talks about the ill-treatment of the native population and his hope of getting an Irish Franciscan Mission sent out as a means of checking the further exploitation of the unfortunate natives. He read me parts of his report and showed me photographs of men, women and children who had been tortured in the most brutal manner.

"Among other things he told me of a diary belonging to one of the worst scoundrels engaged in ill-treating the natives. *He had got possession of this diary and had translated it and sent it to the Foreign Office along with his report* and other papers containing evidence against the Company and its employees."

Mr. P. S. O'Hegarty, late permanent Secretary of the Department of Posts and Telegraphs, has also placed on record in the National Library of Ireland an account which reads:

"He was full of his Putumayo experiences and would speak of nothing else. I asked him about the men responsible for the business. . . He blamed most of all a man called Normand. . . The point about him Casement stressed most was that his European training seemed to have made him more of a devil than any of his associates who had no contact with Europe.

105

"He told me that this man's private diary recorded in his own hand *details of the most unnatural and abominable crimes. He said that he had sent the diary to the Foreign Office and had kept a copy of it.* I cannot clearly recollect now whether the diary went in with his report or subsequent to it, or whether it was the diary went in or the copy. But at any rate there is no doubt that there was extant a copy of this diary in Casement's handwriting, and that this was either at the Foreign Office or amongst Casement's own papers."

Denis Gwynn, in his biography of Roger Casement, says:

"He talked much to his more intimate friends about the evidence he had collected; and it is a curious fact that he mentioned to several of them that among the documents which he was sending to the Foreign Office was a diary of precisely the character which he was afterwards accused of having kept himself."

It is believed that the photostatic extracts which were shown in Washington, New York and London were passages taken out of their context in Armando Normand's diary and passed off as Casement's own. Some of those who knew Casement's handwriting asked no more, but one shrewd New York lawyer, John Quinn, remarked that without the context they were worthless.

The irony of it is that Casement, according to one of the witnesses, thinking the contents too loathsome to be given to a typist, had copied them himself, thus playing directly into the hands of those who made the photostatic copies.

Later Sir Basil Thomson made a most important statement.

"*I have made special inquiry with a view to ascertaining how long Casement has been under the obsessions disclosed in the pages of his diary, and I feel certain that they were of comparatively recent growth, probably not much before the year 1910."* (*Queer People*, p. 92, by Sir Basil Thomson).

What, then, becomes of the diary from 1903?

Sir Basil Thomson had burned, so he says, his own officially typed copy of the complete journal "from 1903 onwards" ("in case it should fall into the hands of my executors"). It was supposed that the other copies had been withdrawn or destroyed, or at any rate that they would not be subject to further inspection. After the execution of Casement Sir Edward Grey had indeed cabled to Washington and to the various consulates his instructions to stop the circulation of the "diaries". Perhaps Sir Basil Thomson overlooked the fact that there survived at least one copy, just that one copy to which reference has so frequently been made in 1956, a copy surreptitiously obtained, and still containing those records from 1903 onwards which Sir Edward Grey found incredible, and which Sir Ernley Blackwell could only explain preposterously (in the most exact sense of that word) as the record of a pathic sensualist who, by Blackwell's own account, had only given free rein to his unnatural appetites at a much later date; as we have seen, Sir Basil Thomson, after "special inquiry", ended in the same preposterous contradiction.

In 1921 F. E. Smith showed the alleged diary to Michael Collins and Eamon Duggan at the time of the negotiations preceding the Irish Treaty. Duggan's description of the contents of the diary shows that it was undoubtedly concerned with the natives of the Putumayo district; and to this extent it confirms the belief of Casement's friends that if it was in Casement's writing it was a manipulated portion of

Casement's translation of Armando Normand's diary. According to one story this was again a typed copy, but according to the story generally received Michael Collins is said to have recognized the handwriting as that of Casement. A few months afterwards he told an Irish friend that "either the writing was that of Casement or an infernally clever copy of it". Collins, therefore, realized the possibility of forgery.

If this be true, then F. E. Smith was able to produce at that time a manuscript diary (in one volume?). How Smith was able to call for its production at short notice, by an attendant in the House of Lords, and from what secret archives, we are not told. With the necessity of smearing Casement in the eyes of his fellow-countrymen, F. E. Smith had naturally provided for that contingency. This was in effect a continuation of the smear campaign deterring straightforward men from making further demands for authentication. And a fine light it throws upon the assertion of the Home Office that it now refuses authentication because, according to its high tradition, after an execution the memory of its victim should not further be blackened by such a disclosure!

Mr. René MacColl states, in a letter to me of May 1st, 1956, that he has seen the complete official copies of "five immense volumes and three ledgers" (quite an undertaking. The addition seems to have been a fairly large one). Moreover, he states that they extend from 1901 *to* 1912. If, as the head of the C.I.D. asserted (the reiteration is necessary), the alleged offences occurred not much before 1910, this leaves only the period between 1910 to the date when the trunks were left in Ebury Street, for the record on which, *and on which alone*, Sir Ernley Blackwell grounded his preposterous Memorandum to the Cabinet that:

"Casement's diary and his ledger entries covering many pages of closely typed matter, show that he has for years been addicted to the grossest sodomitical practices. Of late years he seems to have completed the full cycle of sexual degeneracy. . . No one who has read Casement's report to the Foreign Office on the Putumayo atrocities (*at a time when his sexual offences were of daily occurrence*) . . . could doubt for a moment that Casement intellectually at any rate is very far removed from anything that could properly be described as insanity."

All that one can say to this is that Sir Ernley Blackwell did not know, when he made this abominable statement to the Cabinet, that Sir Basil Thomson was going to publish the report of his "special inquiry"; and that Sir Basil Thomson had no idea that Sir Ernley Blackwell's Memorandum, after submission to the Cabinet, would ever again see the light of day, as it did for the first time in 1956.

It must be repeated again, and with emphasis, that the period referred to was just that period in which Armando Normand comes fully into the picture, and includes the period during which Casement himself was in the constant company of the five representatives of the rubber firm on which he made his devastating report. He was surrounded by the watchful eyes of local enemies, and if the offences attributed to him at this time were of "daily occurrence", is it remotely conceivable that these five witnesses of his life should not have given the slightest hint of it?

The incredibly mean answer given by some upholders of the authenticity of the diary is "Ah, but you see people were so secretive in those days." In other words, if you cannot find anything against a man, he is undoubtedly guilty. And again, the sweet little contradiction between the idea of secretiveness and those five immense diaries described by Mr. René MacColl, recording offences of incredible frequency.

In view of the implications of the diary, perhaps the most contradictory phrase used by Sir Basil Thomson about Casement was the remark after his interrogatory: "*He struck me as an idealist.*"

CHAPTER X

THE CONTRADICTIONS in Sir Ernley Blackwell's statement, not only of the "special inquiry" by the head of the C.I.D., but of a great many other known facts, have been noted by one of Casement's still surviving relatives, Mr. Seamas MacCall, who is certainly qualified to speak for those who knew Casement. He writes:

"I also have the advantage of knowing something of the actual conditions under which Roger worked in Peru. And I can assure your readers that no man in the position of a Consular official in that part of the world could have misconducted himself without it being widely known locally, and without every detail of it being eagerly seized upon and used to discredit him by the agents of the powerful interests which his investigations were threatening to ruin. On the other hand Armando Normand and some of the other Putumayo criminals most certainly *did* misconduct themselves, and Normand most certainly *did* record his exploits in diaries and other documents which Casement translated and submitted to the Foreign Office."

As for the officially typed copies of the alleged diary (or diaries), the only oversight was perhaps that the manipulators retained or included just a little too much of what was genuine. There is a passage, for instance, in which Casement condemns expressly the very perversion with which he is charged, and speaks of it as a "terrible disease". It concerns the suicide of Sir Hector MacDonald, on the eve of his court-martial for a homosexual offence. The passage runs: "The most distressing case surely of its kind, and one that may awake the national mind to saner methods of curing a terrible disease than by criminal legislation." Those who support the authenticity of the diary have two ways of dealing with this passage:

The first is to omit the phrase "a terrible disease" altogether, and to say only that Casement was shocked by the report—which might mean, of course, that he shared those proclivities.

The second, adopted by one of the most ardent champions of the charges against Casement, is to say that the passage proves the incriminating additions to be genuine, for otherwise those responsible for the "discovery" would have erased it. This testimony to honourable men reminds one of Chesterton's verse on the Dreyfus case:

> They gathered all the evidence
> That could remove a doubt.
> They wrote a postcard in his name,
> And partly scratched it out.

So this champion himself confesses involuntarily that the sentence is one which so definitely conflicts with the other charges as to require erasure if those charges are to be substantiated. As a preliminary to this, he takes immense pains to prove, after seeing a *typed* copy, that interpolations were physically impossible, because, he says, on the word of somebody else (unnamed) who claims that he had seen the original, shown to him by a person in authority unnamed, after threats of prosecution if he revealed the truth, that there were no gaps which could be filled up. Of course there were none if they had been already filled up. Interpolations, he says naïvely, would have had to be inserted not only at the end of a paragraph but sometimes in the middle of it. Evidently he thinks that a forger intelligent enough to erase would be incapable of adding a line or two on other subjects, or leaving innocuous entries undisturbed in order to provide the necessary touches of authenticity.

To account for these glaring discrepancies in the diary there is a suggestion that Sir Roger Casement, whose character Conrad and all who knew him found so crystal clear, had a split personality. This will deceive only the gullible. A split personality is one thing—a split diary is quite another. "Ah," says another champion, "but the ink was the same colour; it had faded uniformly." It is of course a well-known fact that expert forgers faking passages in documents invariably use red ink.

It is impossible to reconcile any of these accounts of the faked diary (in themselves all conflicting) with the account of yet another document shown by Admiral Hall to the representative of the Associated Press, Ben S. Allen, a living witness, as part of the original manuscript. His account of it is in the National Library of Ireland at Dublin. It runs:

"Hall showed it to me at first at the conclusion of the regular Wednesday weekly interview with the American correspondents, and told me the Associated Press could have it for exclusive publication if it wished it... The diary was in manuscript in what I recall as finely written in the handwriting of a person of culture and originality.

"I told Hall that, while the A. P. was not interested in scandal for its own sake, because of the importance of the individual and the events in which he was playing such an important role, we might use it. However, I told him it must be authenticated completely before we would use it, and I saw only one way of doing so, and that was by permitting me to show it to Sir Roger Casement then in Pentonville. If he were to acknowledge it as authentic I would then submit the document to my chief in the London Bureau of the A. P. Hall neither assented to nor denied this request, but replaced the manuscript in his desk.

"For several weeks thereafter he showed me the diary repeating the offer, and on each occasion I made the same stipulation. . . Late in the negotiations Hall showed me some typewritten excerpts from the diary, evidently designed to illustrate the innuendo of perversions. Nothing in the copy I read showed anything except the ravings of the victim of perversions.

"I recall my horror at those revelations. I cannot recall that any vigorous effort was made to press the diary on me, but the effort was repeated several times, and it was stated that the contents were of such significance that its publication would prove of great news interest. After the execution of Sir Roger the subject was dropped and I heard of the diary only casually until several years after."

Mr. Allen (as quoted from *Hansard* in my first chapter), wrote to Lieut.-Col. Montgomery Hyde on March 7th, 1956, a letter of which I give an extract:

"That was the only discussion I had with Hall—my insistence that I take the copy of the diary to Casement to get his side of the story. *His repeated refusal convinced me that there was something back of it that he dared not disclose.*"

There is a further account in W. J. Maloney's *The Forged Casement Diaries*. I am mentioned no less than twenty-three times in the index of this book, a fact which may go a long way towards explaining the continued association of my name with the circulation of the diaries, as exemplified by the interjection of Mr. Emrys Hughes recorded on page 23. Mr. Maloney writes:

"Admiral Hall . . . repeatedly showed 'Casement's diary' to Allen. 'It was a rolled manuscript,' writes Allen, 'which Hall took from a pigeon-hole in his desk. . . The paper was buff in colour, with blue lines and the sheets ragged at the top as if they had been torn from what, in my school days, we called a composition book. . . The paper was not quite legal size'." Allen added that he wished to verify authenticity partly because of professional ethics, but also because he knew Casement and this did not fit in with his estimate of the man. (Statement by Allen in the National Library of Ireland in Dublin.)

It is possible that this rolled paper was actually a part of Casement's translation of the Normand diary. This would account for it not being in the *volume* form described by Basil Thomson and others.

We are told nothing of the provenance of these loose leaves, which were certainly not torn from the Letts diaries described by the one man who claims (most unsatisfactorily in the face of the flat denials by the Home Office—the reader can choose between them) to have had sight of the originals.

Some light may be thrown on the detached pages by the evidence of a physician (H. S. Dickey, M.D.) who had been employed by the Peruvian Rubber Company. In 1936, after reading Denis Gwynn's *Life of Casement*, he wrote to the author expressing his conviction that the "infamous diary" was fraudulent. He also made an affidavit before a notary public that he had known Casement well, had accompanied him for several weeks on one of his expeditions and had given him certain information about the iniquities in the Putumayo. Casement forwarded this information to Malet at the Foreign Office but there was also other information bearing on the subject of what Casement had believed to be "a vice of civilization", unknown in Putumayo before the arrival of the white man. Casement had just had some query from Conan Doyle about this and made a number of notes which (according to the physician) might easily have been misrepresented as part of the "diary". Elsewhere he says that Casement was the very last person he would suspect of such offences. Writing as a physician of thirty years' standing he says that "if Casement was one of those unfortunates, I am a rotten diagnostician."

This fits in with what all who knew Casement well have said about him. Dr. H. S. Dickey had no particular reason to feel friendly towards Casement, for the unexpected publication by Casement of certain information about the Company which he had received from the physician made it necessary for the latter to throw up his appointment. He had no motive in making his affidavit (now in the National Library) except to clear Casement. This M.D. (of Boston University) says that he dictated to Casement some lengthy notes of his medical knowledge about native perversions and that Casement remarked "This is awful stuff to entrust to the post." It will be remembered that when Casement was told in Pentonville about the use that was being made of an alleged diary, he at once exclaimed that they could have had nothing against him personally, but must be using some of his Putumayo notes.

This fits in both with Dickey's remark that these notes could have provided photostatic material and with Allen's description of the concentrated nature of the 'erotica' which were shown to him by Hall.

In a former chapter an account has been given of the political background, the tangle of conflicting loyalties and disloyalties both in England and Northern Ireland, which should certainly make more comprehensible what the late Stephen Gwynn called the "duality" of Casement's political position. With this qualification it may be said that Stephen Gwynn, in his estimate of Casement as a man and his condemnation of the campaign of calumny, is perfectly just. Stephen Gwynn was a writer of distinction and outstanding ability. He sat in Parliament for twelve years and had a fine record of service in the 1914 war. In his *Recollections of a Literary Man* he writes:

"His (Roger Casement's) Report on the Congo had not yet attained the immense publicity it received when it made the solid platform which swept the Congo Free State out of being. In that bitter campaign, no weapon was left unused on either side, and if it had been possible to smirch Casement's name by any means, it would have been blackened. Yet he came out from all that propaganda and counter-propaganda famous through Europe, and carrying such prestige that he was the inevitable choice for a similar mission of inquiry into the methods of rubber collecting in the Amazon basin. His report on the Putumayo region carried the most damning authority. Few reputations showed brighter than his, when in 1912 he retired from the Consular Service with a knighthood.

"My interest in African affairs had slackened since Mary

Kingsley's death; but meeting Casement had extraordinary interest for me. Yet what remains now in my mind is chiefly the impression of his personal charm and beauty. It was a superb day in June and most of us were staying at the hotel in that attractive little village by the tideway of the river: he was lodged elsewhere, and came strolling down after dinner, in evening clothes but with a loose coat of grey Irish frieze thrown over them and a straw hat crowning his dark, handsome face with its pointed black beard. Figure and face, he seemed to me then one of the finest-looking creatures I had ever seen; and his countenance had charm and distinction and a high chivalry. Knight-errant he was; clear-sighted, cool-headed, knowing as well as any that ever lived how to strengthen his case by temperate statement, yet always charged with passion.

"Nothing in this life has surprised me more than the tragic evolution of his career. I did not approve of the course by which Eoin MacNeill incurred sentence of death in 1916 for organizing rebellion; but it never perplexed me that Mac-Neill should have done so. But I have never been able to understand the duality of Casement's position. That he should work in the British Consular Service to end an abominable wrong in the Congo, and later on the Putumayo River, did not commit him to any enthusiasm for British rule in Ireland. But even in 1904 he was, I am credibly told, engaged in propaganda against recruiting for the British Army, while still a civil servant; and in 1912 as a member of the Civil Service he accepted an honour from the Government which—in so far as it was the Government of Ireland— he was even then planning to overthrow.

"I do not know how he reconciled the two faces of his

career. But having said that, I say none the less that Roger Casement still seems to me one of those who in my time did real and conspicuous service to humanity, and seems also one of the most noble creatures I have known.

"No fair mind can deny that the British Government was fully entitled to execute him or that many men in authority could have felt it their inevitable duty to carry out that sentence. But the meanest thing I have known to be done by the tools of a Government was the private circulation of statements about his sexual morality, which were calculated to offset the widespread public feeling that it was wrong to hang such a man."

On the eve of the State trial there was a solemn discussion in the Cabinet on the question whether Sir Roger Casement should be found guilty of treason, or "guilty but insane". The Cabinet decided that, in view of his known record and his known and genuine writings, a diagnosis of insanity could not be sustained merely on the basis of the "diary" placed before them by its eager sponsor F. E. Smith and discovered by Sir Basil Thomson (for the year 1903)—which was, according to his own later statement, "after special inquiry", seven years before the offences began. Yet this diary for 1903, according to Sir Basil Thomson's still earlier statement, was "unprintable in any language or at any time". In view of such discrepancies, one can hardly wonder that examination is not allowed!

When the officially typed copy of this diary was submitted to the Cabinet, Sir Edward Grey declared that the very frequency of the alleged acts made the whole thing incredible. We have seen how Sir Ernley Blackwell surmounted his objection.

For those who, unlike Sir Ernley Blackwell, have old-fashioned prejudices, the exact words of his Memorandum to the Cabinet, of July 17th, 1916, as quoted in *Hansard* on May 3rd, 1956, are given on page 17.

It has been said earlier that one of the most damning facts about the varying contradictions in the moral charges brought against Casement is that in every instance there is an obvious motive for each of the falsities invoked. The motive in this instance was plainly to surmount the incredibility, as Sir Edward Grey called it, of the story laid before the Cabinet by F. E. Smith.

And here is another glaring discrepancy, and yet another plain motive to inspire it. According to Sir Ernley Blackwell, the moral degradation of Casement, so completely accomplished in his later years, was the result of a long process of otherwise incredibly frequent acts recorded in the alleged diaries from 1903 onwards (and according to the *typed copy* seen by Mr. MacColl, from 1901 onwards). They were incredibly frequent according to the diaries unless he had *already* reached the stage which (according to Sir Ernley Blackwell) he only reached in later years.

There is another aspect of the incredibility Sir Edward Grey found in the record of those practices "of daily occurrence". If it were true, we must suppose that the British Government had retained in its service for a long period of time a man whose offences were so frequent that they could not possibly have escaped the attention of his associates in that service. Official toleration—and this in the first decades of the century—would have extended to "incredibly frequent" acts in London, Belfast, Lisbon and all the other places mentioned. Yet it was only when it became necessary to discredit Casement politically that F. E. Smith and his collaborators were able to produce exactly what was needed.

Taken together with the timing of the untrue telegram from Copenhagen, preparing the way of the forger and making the crooked path straight, the timing here was a little too perfect—so perfect that Voltaire, in a weak moment, would have called it "providential", and Zola would have underlined it with "J'accuse".

CHAPTER XI

Thou, barely 'scaped from justice,
Take oath to judge the land.

RUDYARD KIPLING.

ENGLAND CONCEDED to Sir Roger Casement a State
trial, and it has been rather smugly proclaimed that he was
allowed the best legal advisers, including Welsh, Irish and
American counsel. It has not been so widely made known
that owing to the methods used for prejudging the case it was
only after many difficulties that a solicitor could be found to
take up the defence. Mr. Gavan Duffy, the solicitor who did
so, was, against all traditions of the English legal profession,
forced to resign from the firm in which he had been a
partner. Although private individuals subscribed generously
to the defence fund (Conan Doyle subscribed £700) the
defence was straitened for lack of funds. The sum promised
for the expenses of the American counsel was not forthcom-
ing, and the most eminent of the lawyers concerned, Professor J. H. Morgan, acted without fee.

At the trial Rufus Isaacs was Presiding Judge.

F. E. Smith, in his capacity of Attorney-General, was able
to appoint himself as Crown Prosecutor of his own political
enemy, and, as H. G. Wells said, it was a "shocking con-
juncture". At the very beginning of his opening address to
the Jury, the Prosecutor made a statement which was belied
(though the Jury could not know it) by the whole history of
Casement's political views on Ireland. Moreover Smith had

THE NAMES ON LIMERICK 1916 MEMORIAL

The Limerick 1916 Memorial, unveiled on Sunday last, has inscribed on it the names of 82 Irish patriots executed by the British or killed in action during the Irish War of Independence. The following is a full official list of the names with the county of birth:—

KILLED IN ACTION.

Dublin: Peadar Macken, Francis Macken, Peter Manning, Michael Malone, Daniel Murray, Richard Murphy, Richard O'Reilly, Thomas O'Reilly, Thomas Rafferty, Frederick Ryan, Peter D'Arcy, Ernest Kavanagh, Donal Murphy, James Byrne, John Kiely, Joseph Kelly, Richard O'Carroll, Sean Connolly, John Corrigan, John Cremin, Joseph Quinn, John Devane, Patrick Doyle, Patrick Whelan, Patrick O'Flanagan, Patrick O'Farrell, John O'Grady, John Healy, John Owens, Sean Howard, Eamonn Walsh, Phillip Walsh, Charles D'Arcy, William Burke, John Adams, Eamonn Ennis, James McCormack, William McDowell, Henry Coyle, Gerald Keogh, Peter Wilson, George Reynolds, John Traynor, Andrew Byrne, Louis Byrne.

Antrim: Charles Monahan.

Kerry: Con Keating, Patrick O'Connor, Michael Mulvihill, John O'Reilly, The O'Rahilly, Patrick Shortice.

Meath: Philip Walsh, Thomas Allen, James Fox.

Limerick: Donal Sheehan.

Cork: Richard Kent (killed in action in Fermoy), John Hurley.

Carlow: Margaret Keogh.

Kildare: George Geoghegan.

Galway: Brendan Donnellan.

Glasgow: Charles Corrigan.

Westmeath: John Costelloe.

Wexford: James Corcoran, Thomas Weafer.

England: Arthur Weeks (killed in action in Dublin).

THE EXECUTIONS IN KILMAINHAM.

Executed by the British in Kilmainham Prison:

Thomas Clarke, James Connolly, Eamonn Kent, Con Colbert, Edward Daly, Sean Heuston, Sean MacDiarmada, Michael Mallin, John McBride, Thomas McDonagh, Joseph Plunkett, Michael O'Hanrahan, William Pearse, Patrick Pearse.

Executed by the British in Cork Prison: Thomas Kent.

Executed in London: Roger Casement.

the knowledge that the excerpts from the diaries, which, through Travers Humphreys, he had offered to the defending counsel, with the suggestion that, by an admission of their authenticity, the prosecution might co-operate with the defence to put his political opponent in a lunatic asylum, must have placed the defence at a psychological disadvantage. The offer of this co-operation was ingenious as it was base. It would avoid the danger afterwards discussed in the Cabinet that a man executed for treason might become a patriot-martyr.

It would also involve a most improper collusion between prosecution and defence, and also between prosecution and the judges, to maintain the charge of insanity (in which none of them believed and which the Cabinet subsequently decided could not be maintained in law). It is sometimes said that F. E. Smith made this proposal because he wished to save Casement's life. As for this, Smith actually brought political pressure to bear on the Cabinet by threatening that he would resign unless Casement were hanged.

In an interview in 1918 with the *Boston Post* he said:

"In the first place it does not seem to be known here that after the trial of Sir Roger Casement I threatened to resign from the Cabinet unless this traitor was executed. You will remember that a tremendous effort was made to save Casement and for a time the Government was wobbling. *I gave them choice of Casement or myself.* Nothing gave me greater delight than the execution of Casement." (*Boston Post*, January 14th, 1918.)

If this is true Smith must have had a miserable life!

But although the prosecution was refused the co-operation of the defence, the atmosphere was poisoned by rumours

123

about the diaries, and there was one bit of play-acting in Court which might indirectly help the smear campaign. Evidence was given that when Casement landed in Tralee Bay there was found, in what was ostentatiously called a "black bag", where he and his two companions landed, a single sheet of paper with a few dates scribbled upon it, in an unidentified handwriting, apparently the dates of recent journeys and embarkations. The policemen who found it testified that it was a single sheet of paper, and added: "it looked like a kind of diary." F. E. Smith fastened on this word and the single sheet of paper was not referred to again, but a curious bit of play-acting followed in Court:

"THE LORD CHIEF JUSTICE: Mr. Attorney, you mentioned a passage in the *diary*. Is there any evidence as to whose *diary* it is?

"THE ATTORNEY-GENERAL: It was a *diary*. I will give your Lordship the evidence of it. It was a *diary found*.

"THE LORD CHIEF JUSTICE: I know. But as far as my recollection goes there was no further evidence given beyond the fact that it was found. Whose writing it is, or whose *diary* it is, there is no evidence.

"THE ATTORNEY-GENERAL: My Lord, I did not say it was a *diary* of any particular person. I said '*the diary*'. By *the diary* I mean the *diary* which was *found* and is in evidence as having been *found*.

"THE LORD CHIEF JUSTICE: I thought it right to indicate that, because it might have conveyed to the Jury that it was *Casement's diary*. There is no evidence of it.

"THE ATTORNEY-GENERAL: You have heard, gentlemen (of

the Jury) what my Lord has said. If there was any misunderstanding I am glad it should be removed."

Remove the misunderstanding! The misunderstanding was deliberately contrived, with a most cunning and elaborate misuse of associated ideas for the benefit of the jury and of the public who had already heard rumours of a *diary found*. Even a historian like Denis Gwynn, in his book *The Life and Death of Roger Casement*, was led into a doubt whether the alleged black diary or diaries were found in a locked trunk at Ebury Street or where Casement had landed at Tralee Bay. If it could mislead Professor Gwynn, it could certainly mislead a not too analytical public and jury.

In this one brief passage, it will be noted, the word "diary" is used ten times. When F. E. Smith was pretending to clarify the matter by saying what he meant by "the diary", why did he omit any reference to the single sheet of paper? Why did he not say "By the diary I mean the single sheet of paper with the brief itinerary and disguised names and places, which was in evidence as having been found on the beach"? Why did he merely reiterate the word which would not normally be applied to a sheet of paper and would certainly suggest to most people a book? Why did he simply say: "I said 'the diary'. By 'the diary' I mean the diary which was found", an association of ideas continued by the judicious interruption of Rufus Isaacs, "*I know*", and his subsequent most judiciously deprecatory remark: "It might have conveyed to the jury that it was *Casement's diary*. There is no evidence of that." No, but the very use of the phrase "Casement's diary" without clarification would, in a great many minds, imply the existence of that other "diary"—a subtle reminder of something that should not be brought into Court but had been gossiped about in the world outside. Casement's diary! If it be true that a scrap of paper once involved the honour of a great nation, the treatment of this other scrap of paper certainly involved the honour of an Attorney-General and several others. The word "diary" was hammered into the public mind with all the energy of a commercial advertisement breaking into a radio programme. If the reader had any doubt about the iniquity of this proceeding, let him turn again to F. E. Smith's *Famous Trials*. Here, despite what the Lord Chief Justice had said about the misunderstanding, he states without any qualification whatever, that Casement's diary was found in the pocket of a coat abandoned near the ruined fort on the Tralee coast.

The jury, in an atmosphere poisoned with gossip about Casement's alleged diary, must certainly have been misled by this piece of deliberate *suggestio falsi*.

It will be noted that F. E. Smith's account in *Famous Trials* completely annihilates the judicious observation with which Rufus Isaacs both deprecated and subtly confirmed the "misunderstanding".

Wisely and frankly, the present Lord Birkenhead, in his life of F. E. Smith, makes atonement for the parental mistake by saying there were found in the sand "three coats, in the pocket of one of which was found a railway ticket from Berlin to Wilhelmshaven". This is the correct version of what was "given in evidence" and listed by the police.

In an introduction to the verbatim report of the Casement trial, the Editor, Mr. G. H. Knott, tells us that the Attorney-General had revised his own speech for the prosecution. It is a pity he did not revise Mr. Knott's preface, in which,

126

alluding to F. E. Smith's association with Carson's army and its invocation of German military aid, he unashamedly remarks:

"There was *piquancy* in the fact that the Attorney-General had taken so prominent a part in the Ulster movement, and that Casement appealed to the movement as an excuse for his treason."

Piquancy! Strange word to describe a fact which, although it could not be brought into any merely legal aspect of the case unless as proof of the most intense provocation, involved as nauseating a transgression and travesty of real justice as has ever been enacted in a court of law. Here was a man standing in the dock, the fulfillment of whose dreams for his native country had been granted by a Bill in the British House of Commons; and who had seen those dreams and aspirations wrecked by his prosecutor's appeal to arms and German aid; and he was now facing death at the hands of his political enemy for the counter-measure into which he had been misled and actually taunted. "The Nationalists will neither fight for it nor pay for it." The very words of the man who now claimed the forfeit of the accused man's life. Piquancy!

A few points should be made clear. As far as the political charges were concerned, the only marked difference between Casement's words and actions and those of his prosecutor in the fomenting of rebellion in Ulster, was in the not infrequent nobility of the prisoner's thoughts and words. Contrast, for instance, Casement's noble speech from the dock with the sneering vulgarity of F. E. Smith's interjection as he ostentatiously lounged out of Court in the middle of it. "Change places with *him*? Nothing doing!" The ejaculation was against all the decencies of legal procedure, and doubly indecent as coming from the Attorney-General, vulgarly interrupting a declaration which will go down in history.

The incident gives a sharp point to those words of a man already pre-judged and pre-condemned. "There is not a glint or gleam of chivalry in all their battle-line." If there had been one spark of generous humanity in the prosecutor he might have realized, and even humbly realized, that his victim was a man whose rebellion was not against his own country, but on behalf of what he sincerely felt to be his own beloved and grievously wronged people.

Even more indecent was the prosecutor's interference with the prerogative of mercy, in bringing political pressure to bear upon the Government of the day against the granting of a reprieve. This he did at the moment when Lord Crewe was endeavouring to draw the attention of the Cabinet to the ample evidence of Casement's desperate attempt to prevent the Easter Rising (this plea was not an after-thought; the record of his attempts and the consequent German anger and derision is in the Munich diary). There is no doubt that Lord Crewe was right, and that the letter which he laid before them from Eva Gore-Booth gave a true account of Casement's intention. It is borne out by the report which the rebels themselves sent to Devoy in America—that a message had been sent to them from Casement begging them to defer the Rising until he arrived. His intention (as was shown earlier), was to dissuade them from useless bloodshed. Basil Thomson himself speaks of this message to Devoy in his *Queer People*, page 95.

Further confirmation may be found in the fact that immediately after his arrest Casement, although a Protestant, asked that he might be put in touch with a Catholic priest, whom he entreated to "tell the Volunteers in the town and elsewhere to keep perfectly quiet. Tell them that I am a prisoner, and that the rebellion will be a dismal, hopeless failure, as the help they expect will not arrive." The priest (Father F. M. Ryan) gave the message and later confirmed this by letter to Gavan Duffy, Casement's solicitor.

The culmination of indecency was in F. E. Smith's statement that nothing gave him greater delight than the hanging of a fellow-creature, an expression that may justly be compared with the cheers of the gutter-snipes at the tolling of the prison bell, while the Irish were kneeling in prayer outside the prison gates.

At the trial Casement's counsel, Serjeant Sullivan, broke down in Court and had to be replaced by his junior. On the charge of treason the real defence, which depended entirely on the political background described in earlier chapters, was only partly formulated. Serjeant Sullivan made the attempt, but when he came to the real point he was foiled by the smooth intervention of Rufus Isaacs, who, as Lord Chief Justice of England, naturally had a fellow feeling for an Attorney-General in danger.[1] Here is the crucial part of what Serjeant Sullivan said:

"There is an enormous mass of testimony of different men speaking of different speeches and many of them at different times, and a most extraordinary thing about it is, as far as I have read, Sir Roger Casement's speeches were obviously all of them on the same line, that the Irish Brigade was being formed, and would remain at Berlin under Irish officers in

---

[1] Three years earlier, F. E. Smith had been briefed as one of the two leading counsel for Rufus Isaacs in two cases arising out of the Marconi scandals. The other leading counsel, incidentally, was Carson.

Irish uniform, the guests and not the servants of Germany.
When the war was over, if Germany won they were to be
landed in Ireland. Under no circumstances were they to be
asked to fight for any country except their own. They were
to be landed in Ireland, and in Ireland alone was the Irish
Brigade to be used if their use became necessary. . . . There
is a most extraordinary cohesion of separate stories told by
different men that the Irish Brigade was being recruited on
a solemn undertaking and that they were appealed to as
Irishmen to enter into the service of their own country, they
were never to be the servants of any other nation, they were
not to be the servants of Germany, and they were under no
circumstances to be used for any German end. You will bear
that in mind because, as I told you before, you will see how
you will have to deal with that as showing what was in Sir
Roger Casement's mind."

Serjeant Sullivan then dealt with the evidence of the Irish
soldiers who, under an exchange arrangement, had been
brought over from Germany to be witnesses at the trial.
They were all men who had refused to join the Irish Brigade,
and were therefore, in themselves, an answer to the charge
that those who refused to join were sent to the worst places
in Germany. All, with one exception, agreed with Serjeant
Sullivan's contention. It is a remarkable fact, and in accord-
ance with a hundred other facts throughout this whole affair,
that the only one of these witnesses whose evidence favoured
the contention of the prosecution was proved under cross-
examination to be so extremely unreliable that the prosecution itself was forced eventually to repudiate him. All,
except the last-named witness, testified to the fact that when
their rations were reduced it was on dates of universal

reduction throughout the camp. This of course was due to the efficient work of the British Navy.

Serjeant Sullivan continued:

"What was there in Ireland in 1914 and 1915 purporting to act in the name of England that required to be fought to secure Home Rule? I would be most unwilling to say anything that might in the slightest degree seem to be trespassing or infringing on the opinions of any person in this Court or outside it, but you will have to answer that question and look back and seek to find upon the evidence what was the power that called itself England in Ireland in 1914, for, as I have already pointed out, under the constitution there is no English power in Ireland. You have got a glimpse from two or three or four witnesses of the state of affairs existing in that country, almost within gunshot of your own country, that casts a reflection and a disgrace upon our civilization. *It is a dreadful thing, gentlemen, a dreadful thing to contemplate that anyone within the King's peace in any part of his United Kingdom should be subjected to the bullying and intimidation and threat of armed force to be exercised against the liberties secured to him by the constitution and by the Parliament of Great Britain and Ireland; and yet such was the state of affairs in Ireland as you see by the evidence.* What was the necessity of arming men in Ireland? As one witness says, to secure Home Rule, another to free Ireland, another to secure the freedom of Ireland. To protect the liberties of Ireland against whom had you to arm? Was there in Ireland in those years an armed body which most improperly used the name of your country behind which to shelter the invasion of the liberties secured to Irishmen under the constitution? You have evidence that there was, unless indeed you believe, being constitutionally

ignorant in this Court of what barbarous law may in fact
prevail beyond the Channel—unless indeed you would
assume from the immunity with which armed bands
paraded the country north and south for the avowed purpose
of attacking one another sooner or later, unless you believe
from this immunity that these things may be done under the
laws in Ireland, and that we who desire to live in peace and
to possess what we are entitled to, our own opinions, may
not form them in Ireland save at the bayonet's point of some
faction or other. Does not that show you in one gleam what
it was that Sir Roger Casement was doing in Limburg when
he recruited the Irish Brigade? Observe the state of affairs
as you have proved it in evidence. There was in the north of
Ireland an armed body of men ostensibly marching about, as
Robinson proves, in Belfast, deliberately originated with the
avowed object of resisting the operation of an Act of Parliament which had the approval of the rest of the country. They
armed, and nothing was said to them; they drilled, and nothing was said to them; they marched and counter-marched;
the authorities stood by and looked at them. The police were
powerless. They had great forces behind them, great names
and men of high position. Imagine the feeling in the country
testified to, reaching as far south as what we anciently called
the Kingdom of Kerry, now County Kerry. To the County
of Kerry, in dread of these men, there came a rumour of the
police being powerless, the civil power being paralysed, the
civil government practically abdicated—there came a
rumour that all that stood between peace and the rifles of
those men, His Majesty's Army, might not perhaps be relied
upon. . .

"That gentlemen, is the case that I present to you on

behalf of Sir Roger Casement; that is the explanation of everything that he has done. What is to be said against him? Gentlemen, this condition of affairs had indeed been reached prior to this war that has broken out with the Empire of Germany. There was indeed an understanding and a convention between the greater leaders of these factions arming and counter-arming that for a while, while the danger to the Empire existed, this dreadful state of affairs should be put an end to; that, in the meantime, faith has been kept let us all thank Providence, for it enabled my countrymen, in the service of Ireland, for they are serving the glorious traditions of their own land, to write their names in every battlefield in Europe, a thing that would have been impossible without such understanding. Do not imagine, though you may live in a great city of the Empire, that you can sneer at the loyal patriotism of these men. We recruited none of them to fight for England; no man ever made such an appeal as that to an Irish audience. Each man went forth believing that in serving in this war, he was in truth rendering the best service he could to his own little country. But how about at home? If you are indeed to scrutinize the intention of Sir Roger Casement in what he did abroad, not by what he intended or what was passing in his mind, but the profit the German politicians might calculate that they might ultimately get out of it, you might go back and find that German calculations do not all come right, for you might well think that the enterprising country that filled Ulster with Mausers in 1914 expected a better dividend than she got. The truce was kept in the main, but, gentlemen, not a single rifle was given up. As we have heard from the witnesses, so far from armaments ceasing, on the 16th August the sole obstacle to the importation of arms into Ireland was dropped immediately after the outbreak of the war. *No arms were given up—more arms were coming in...* Well, the arms were still there, the purpose still undisavowed. The truce was on the face of it but a temporary arrangement, a postponement of the threat of bloodshed and outrage which was promised to the country when the war was over; and can you blame that there were found in Ireland fortunately a minority of Irishmen who thought, and, as far as formula goes they thought right, that their first duty of loyalty was to the land of their birth, but who thought that she was still in danger while the country remained divided in armed camps, and there was only to be postponed until the war ended the time when Ireland was to become the foundation for two hells? Many may have thought so honestly and loyally; we who differ from them have no right to criticize their judgment because we disagree with it. They have a right to think, and such men have a right if in their judgment the country was in danger, that it was better to stay at home and provide against this ultimate happening than it was to go forth and serve in the Irish Brigades; men have a right to think that, and in view of the dreadful state of affairs which you have established in evidence before you, how can you blame a man for thinking that; and accordingly there were found men who, distrusting the truce proclaimed in Ireland, seeing that one man would observe his neighbour had not given up his rifle, another that another had got a new gun, he would arm himself, and one by one in small quantities you have the danger of the arms still coming in, and people fearing that the truce was not real, and that at any moment there might break out——

"THE LORD CHIEF JUSTICE: Where is there evidence of that?[1]

"MR. SULLIVAN: The evidence of the Sergeant and the evidence of Robinson.

"THE LORD CHIEF JUSTICE: Of what you are now saying?

"THE ATTORNEY-GENERAL: I was most loath to intervene, but I have heard a great many statements which are wholly uncorroborated.

"THE LORD CHIEF JUSTICE: You have the right to intervene.

"THE ATTORNEY-GENERAL: Statements as to the importation of rifles into the north of Ireland.

"THE LORD CHIEF JUSTICE: We have allowed you very great latitude. I confess for myself I have found it rather difficult not to intervene on several occasions, and I intervene at this moment because I think you are stating matter which is not in evidence or which I have no recollection of being stated in evidence. I know the general passages to which you refer.

"MR. SULLIVAN: I am exceedingly sorry your Lordship did not intervene sooner; I was referring to the evidence of Sergeant Hearn. I am exceedingly sorry I have gone outside what I ought, but what I was referring to was this—

" 'Do you remember in 1914, before the war, the Arms Proclamation?—Yes.

" 'As an officer of the Constabulary were you concerned in acting under it for a while?—Yes.

" 'Prior to that had there been considerable importation of arms?—Yes.

" 'Was it in consequence of what happened in the north

---

[1] Serjeant Sullivan's statements were completely confirmed by the Report of the Royal Commission on the Rebellion in Ireland. *V.* Appendix.

of Ireland that the people were arming as far south as Tralee?—I could not say as to that.

" 'Did they, at all events, purport to be arming?—They did.

" 'As against the armed persons in the north of Ireland? —Yes.

" 'Were they bearing arms openly?—They were.

" 'Without interference by the public authorities?—Yes.

" 'And actually on the outbreak of war was the proclamation against the importation of arms withdrawn on the 16th August?—Yes, that is so.

" 'And your directions, even so far as they went to interfere with the importation of arms, ceased on the 16th August on the withdrawal of the proclamation for the time being?—Yes.

" 'And the arming of the population went on then unrestricted for a while?—Yes.

" 'And the parade of arms uninterfered with by any authority?—Yes.

" 'People drilling?—Yes.

" 'Marching?—Yes.

" 'Skirmishing through the country?—Yes.

" 'Without any action taken on behalf of the police? This arming, of course, commenced before the war, did it not?—Yes, it did.

" 'It commenced some time in 1913 in the south, did it not?—Yes.

" 'It had commenced earlier in the north?—Yes.

" 'Was there a great deal of excitement in the south with regard to what was going on in the north of Ireland? —There was.

" 'I suppose at the police barracks, even in Ardfert, they read the papers?—Yes.' "

Then the papers referred to.

"THE LORD CHIEF JUSTICE: If you look at the question I put, I think it brings home the point of my intervention now. I put to you the question after you had gone through this matter: 'Are you speaking of before or after the war?' and your answer was, 'Before the war.'

"MR. SULLIVAN: That is so with regard to that evidence.

"THE LORD CHIEF JUSTICE: No doubt you stated it quite rightly. You have stated the effect of the facts before the war, and there has been no intervention, but what you are dealing with now apparently is the period some time after the war; the period with which we have to deal is 1915; that is what we are dealing with.

"MR. SULLIVAN: It is this question.

" 'In that state of affairs, having neither police nor military competent to protect one, it was left to people in Ireland to protect themselves; is not that the truth of it?— Generally speaking it is.

" 'Generally speaking that was the truth of it. Now, as you say, when the war broke out the Arms Proclamation was withdrawn and the arming went on as before?—Yes.

" 'And continued right up to last month?—Yes.

" 'Except so far as hampered by the Defence of the Realm regulations?—Yes.'

"I was under the impression I was referring to that. I am sorry if I transgressed, and regret that the rein was not applied to it.

"THE LORD CHIEF JUSTICE: I felt so anxious not to interfere when you were making your speech, and, of course doing the best you could for your client, but you were dealing with matters which not only were not stated in evidence—but with regard to which I will say nothing more."

There was indeed no need for him to say any more. Acting strictly within what may be called the etiquette of legal procedure, and, one might almost say, acting as counsel for the guilty prosecutor, he had blotted out all human considerations, robbing the victim of his only defence and condemning him to death with that real defence unheard—while the condemned man's counsel had to apologize with bated breath for having dared to suggest it. The refusal of Rufus Isaacs, Lord Chief Justice of England, to allow any consideration of the provocation, which had been deliberately designed provocation and advised by men of high position in England for that very purpose (see p. 135), left Sullivan, an exhausted counsel, facing a stone wall on which sentence of death for his client was already written. A very few moments later Serjeant Sullivan, at the end of his tether, was unable to continue, and could only add: "I regret, my Lord, to say that I have completely broken down."

A man's life was at stake, but the most intense provocation, the most extenuating circumstances and every human factor in the case apparently counted for nothing as against the narrowest and strictest interpretation of the rules of legal procedure.

It was easy enough, of course, to say, as F. E. Smith did in his closing speech, that the armed rebellion of Carson and Smith and their associates, with their threats of German aid, took place before the war actually broke out. It did—with only a very short time to spare for calling their "truce".

The words used by Smith about the truce were mere hypocrisy. It was only after they had got what they wanted, a temporary annulment (by a show of armed force) that they dropped their threat of transferring their allegiance to another power; but, as Serjeant Sullivan showed, and as the word "truce" itself implies, their illegally armed force had not been disbanded and it remained as a threat to be used against the supporters of the measure when the truce ended later on.

And as for the shield interposed by Rufus Isaacs between the Attorney-General and the defence, to cover the Attorney-General, the only words appropriate are perhaps these, on one whom there had been shown

> "the reason
> To keep a matter hid,
> And subtly lead the question
> Away from what he did."

Casement's fatal attempt at a counter-action in the South with the Irish Volunteers was also begun *before* the outbreak of the war, but he was already involved when the war came and had taken an irretrievable step. It was one of those cases in which, as in a Greek tragedy:

> "The first step is with us, then all the road,
> The long road, is with fate."

Smith, Carson and their associates had illegitimately secured what they wanted. The Southern Irish, for whom Casement stood, had been robbed of the measure constitutionally passed, and what are we to say of those who, having

139

initiated the whole process of wrong by which this highly-strung idealist was tempted to fight them, could now say to him in his helpless defeat: "You took a desperate hazard. You played and you lost. We now claim the forfeit of your life"? That is how his triumphant political opponent opened his chivalrous case.

The grotesque concentration, with a magnifying glass, on the exact interpretation of a sentence in a mediaeval statute written in Norman-French, was horribly like a satirical scene by Swift, illustrated by Hogarth, and all the more monstrous in a case which was essentially one calling for real human understanding. A comma? Or a crack in the paper? That was the question at one point.

After the verdict had been given Casement was asked, in the usual formula, if he had anything to say before sentence of death was pronounced, and he then made the historic affirmation of which I give here the essential parts. "As he made it," wrote H. W. Nevinson, who was present, "he looked by far the noblest man in Court."

It acquires its full significance only when its neglected background is remembered as it ought to be in any just view. The utter falsehood of the descriptions of it in the gutter-press, which called it the "silly and fatuous statement" of a "paltry traitor", is as contemptible as the more subtle belittlement of recent years. The fact remains that the speech will never be forgotten.[1]

---

[1] Many years later the present Lord Birkenhead (the Attorney-General's son) wrote: "The case seemed suddenly to have achieved the issue of a personal collision. . . . His [Casement's] last words were woven into rare beauty and pathos, and their richness and passion are hardly less moving than the last speech of Strafford three centuries ago." (*Frederick Edwin, Earl of Birkenhead*, by his son, the Earl of Birkenhead.)

"My Lord Chief Justice: . . . The argument that I am now going to read is addressed not to this Court, but to my own countrymen.

"There is an objection, possibly not good in law, but surely good on moral grounds, against the application to me here of this old English statute, 565 years old, that seeks to deprive an Irishman to-day of life and honour, not for 'adhering to the King's enemies', but for adhering to his own people.

"When this statute was passed, in 1351, what was the state of men's minds on the question of a far higher allegiance—that of a man to God and His Kingdom? The law of that day did not permit a man to forsake his church or deny his God save with his life. The 'heretic' then had the same doom as the 'traitor'.

"To-day a man may forswear God and His heavenly kingdom without fear or penalty, all earlier statutes having gone the way of Nero's edicts against the Christians, but that constitutional phantom 'The King' can still dig up from the dungeons and torture chambers of the dark ages a law that takes a man's life for an exercise of conscience.

"If true religion rests on love, it is equally true that loyalty rests on love. The law I am charged under has no parentage in love, and claims the allegiance of to-day on the ignorance and blindness of the past.

"I am being tried, in truth, not by my peers of the live present, but by the peers of the dead past; not by the civilization of the twentieth century, but by the brutality of the fourteenth; not even by a statute framed in the language of an enemy land—so antiquated is the law that must be sought to-day to slay an Irishman whose offence is that he puts Ireland first.

141

"Loyalty is a sentiment, not a law. It rests on love, not on restraint. The Government of Ireland by England rests on restraint and not on law, and since it demands no love it can evoke no loyalty.

"But this statute is more absurd even than it is antiquated; and if it is potent to hang one Irishman, it is still more potent to gibbet all Frenchmen.

"Edward III was King not only of the realm of England but also of the realm of France, and he was not King of Ireland. Yet his dead hand to-day may pull the noose around the Irishman's neck whose Sovereign he was not, but it can strain no strand around the Frenchman's throat whose Sovereign he was. . .

"I did not land in England; I landed in Ireland. It was to Ireland I came; to Ireland I wanted to come; and the last place I desired to land was in England. But for the Attorney-General of England there is only 'England'—there is no Ireland, there is only the law of England—no right of Ireland; the liberty of Ireland and of Irishmen is to be judged by the power of England. . .

"If I did wrong in making that appeal to Irishmen to join with me in an effort to fight for Ireland, it is by Irishmen, and by them alone, that I can be rightfully judged. . . Place me before a jury of my own countrymen, be it Protestant or Catholic, Unionist or Nationalist, Sinn Feineach or Orangemen and I shall accept the verdict and bow to the statute and all its penalties. . .

"I hope I shall be acquitted of presumption if I say that the Court I see before me now is not this High Court of Justice of England; but a far greater, a far higher, a far older assemblage of justices, that of the people of Ireland. Since in the acts which have led to this trial it was the people of Ireland I sought to serve—and them alone—I leave my judgment and my sentence in their hands.

"Let me pass from myself and my own fate to a far more pressing, as it is a far more urgent theme—not the fate of the individual Irishman who may have tried and failed, but the claims and the fate of the country that has not failed. Ireland has outlived the failure of all her hopes—and yet she still hopes. Ireland has seen her sons—aye and her daughters too—suffer from generation to generation, always for the same cause, meeting always the same fate, and always at the hands of the same power, and always a fresh generation has passed on to withstand the same oppression. For if English authority be omnipotent—a power, as Mr. Gladstone phrased it, that reaches to the very ends of the earth— Irish hopes exceed the dimensions of that power, excel its authority, and renew with each generation the claims of the last. The cause that begets this indomitable persistency, the faculty of preserving through centuries of misery the remembrance of lost liberty, this is surely the noblest cause man ever strove for, ever lived for, ever died for. If this be the cause I stand here to-day indicted for, and convicted of sustaining, then I stand in a goodly company and a right noble succession.

"My counsel has referred to the Ulster Volunteer movement, and I will not touch at length upon that ground save only to say this, that neither I nor any of the leaders of the Irish Volunteers who were founded in Dublin in November, 1913, had quarrel with the Ulster Volunteers as such, who were born a year earlier. Our movement was not directed against them, but against the men who misused and misdirected the courage, the sincerity and the local patriotism

143

of the men of the north of Ireland. . . . It was not we, the Irish Volunteers, who broke the law, but a British party. The Government had permitted the Ulster Volunteers to be armed by Englishmen, to threaten not merely an English party in its hold on office, but to threaten that party through the lives and blood of Irishmen. *The battle was to be fought in Ireland in order that the political 'outs' of to-day should be the 'ins' of to-morrow in Great Britain. A law designed for the benefit of Ireland was to be met, not on the floor of Parliament, where the fight had indeed been won, but on the field of battle much nearer home*, where the armies would be composed of Irishmen slaying each other for some English party gain; and the British Navy would be the chartered 'transports' that were to bring to our shores a numerous assemblage of military and ex-military experts. . . . Our choice lay in submitting to foreign lawlessness or resisting it, and we did not hesitate to choose. But while the law-breakers had armed their would-be agents openly, and had been permitted to arm them openly, we were met, within a few days of the founding of our movement, that aimed at uniting Ireland from within, by Government action from without directed against our obtaining arms at all. The Manifesto of the Irish Volunteers, promulgated at a public meeting in Dublin on 25th November, 1913, stated with sincerity the aims of the organization as I have outlined them. If the aims contained in that manifesto were a threat to the unity of the British Empire, then so much the worse for the Empire. An Empire that can only be held together by one section of its governing population perpetually holding down and sowing dissension among a smaller but none the less governing section, must have some canker at its heart, some ruin at its root. The Government that permitted the arming of those whose leaders declared that Irish national unity was a thing that should be opposed by force of arms, within nine days of our manifesto of goodwill to Irishmen of every creed and class, took steps to nullify our efforts by prohibiting the import of all arms into Ireland as if it had been a hostile and blockaded coast. And this proclamation of the 4th December, 1913, known as the Arms Proclamation, was itself based on an illegal interpretation of the law, as the Chief Secretary has now publicly confessed. The proclamation was met by the loyalists of Great Britain with an act of still more lawless defiance—an act of wide-spread gun-running into Ulster that was denounced by the Lord Chancellor of England as 'grossly illegal and utterly unconstitutional'. How did the Irish Volunteers meet the incitements of civil war that were uttered by the party of law and order in England when they saw the prospect of deriving political profit to themselves from bloodshed among Irishmen?

"I can answer for my own acts and speeches. While one English party was responsible for preaching a doctrine of hatred designed to bring about civil war in Ireland, the other, and that the party in power, took no active steps to restrain a propaganda that found its advocates in the Army, Navy and Privy Council—in the Houses of Parliament and in the State Church—a propaganda the methods of whose expression were so 'grossly illegal and utterly unconstitutional' that even the Lord Chancellor of England could only find words and no repressive action to apply to them. Since lawlessness sat in high places in England, and laughed at the law as at the custodians of the law, what wonder was it that Irishmen should refuse to accept the verbal protestations of an English Lord Chancellor as a sufficient safeguard for their lives and their liberties? . . .

"Since arms were so necessary to make our organization a reality, and to give to the minds of Irishmen menaced with the most outrageous threats a sense of security, it was our bounden duty to get arms before all else. I decided with this end in view to go to America, *with surely a better right to appeal to Irishmen there for help in an hour of great national trial than those envoys of 'Empire' could assert for their week-end descents upon Ireland, or their appeals to Germany.* If, as the right honourable gentleman, the present Attorney-General, asserted in a speech at Manchester, Nationalists would neither fight for Home Rule nor pay for it, it was our duty to show him that we knew how to do both. Within a few weeks of my arrival in the States, the fund that had been opened to secure arms for the Volunteers of Ireland amounted to many thousands of pounds. In every case the money subscribed, whether it came from the purse of the wealthy man or the still readier pocket of the poor man, was Irish gold.

"Then came the war. As Mr. Birrell said in his evidence recently laid before the Commission of Inquiry into the causes of the late rebellion in Ireland, 'the war upset all our calculations'. It upset mine no less than Mr. Birrell's, and put an end to my mission of peaceful effort in America. War between Great Britain and Germany meant, as I believed, ruin for all the hopes we had founded on the enrolment of the Irish Volunteers. A constitutional movement in Ireland is never very far from a breach of the constitution, as the loyalists of Ulster had been so eager to show us. The cause is not far to seek. A constitution to be maintained intact must be the achievement and the pride of the people themselves; must rest on their own free will and on their own determination to sustain it, instead of being something resident in another land whose chief representative is an armed force, armed not to protect the population, but to hold it down. *We had seen the working of the Irish constitution in the refusal of the army of occupation at the Curragh to obey the orders of the Crown. And now that we were told that the duty of an Irishman was to enter that army, in return for a promissory note, payable after death—a scrap of paper that might or might not be redeemed, I felt over there in America that my first duty was to keep Irishmen at home in the only army that could safeguard our national existence.*

"If small nationalities were to be the pawns in this game of embattled giants, I saw no reason why Ireland should shed her blood in any cause but her own, and if that be treason beyond the seas I am not ashamed to avow it or to answer for it here with my life. And when we had the doctrine of Unionist loyalty at last—'Mausers and Kaisers and any King you like', and I have heard that at Hamburg, not far from Limburg on the Lahn—I felt I needed no other warrant than what these words conveyed—to go forth and do likewise. The difference between us was that the Unionist champions chose a path they felt would lead to the woolsack, while I went a road I knew must lead to the dock. And the event proves we both were right. The difference between us was that my 'treason' was based on a ruthless sincerity that forced me to attempt in time and season to carry out in action what I said in word—whereas their treason lay in verbal incitements that they knew need never be made good in their bodies. And so, I am prouder to stand here to-day in the traitor's dock to answer this impeachment than to fill the place of my right honourable accusers.

"We have been told, we have been asked to hope, that after this war Ireland will get Home Rule. . . It is not necessary to climb the painful stairs of Irish history—to . . . review the long list of British promises made only to be broken—of Irish hopes raised only to be dashed to the ground. Home Rule when it comes, if come it does, will find an Ireland drained of all that is vital to its very existence— unless it be that unquenchable hope we build on the graves of the dead. . .

"Self-government is our right, a thing born in us at birth; a thing no more to be doled out to us by another people or withheld from us by another people than the right to life itself—than the right to feel the sun or smell the flowers, or to love our kind. . . Where all your rights become only an accumulated wrong; where men must beg with bated breath for leave to subsist in their own land, to think their own thoughts, to sing their own songs, to garner the fruits of their own labours—and even while they beg, to see things inexorably withdrawn from them—then surely it is a braver, a saner and truer thing, to be a rebel in act and deed against such circumstances as these, than tamely to accept it as the natural lot of men.

"My Lord, I have done. Gentlemen of the jury, I wish to thank you for your verdict. I hope you will not take amiss what I have said, or think I made any imputation upon your truthfulness or your integrity when I spoke and said this was not a trial by my peers. I maintain that I have a natural right to be tried in that natural jurisdiction, Ireland, my own country, and I would put it to you, how would you feel in the converse case, or rather how would all men here feel in the converse case, if an Englishman had landed here in

England, and the Crown or the Government, for its own purposes, had conveyed him secretly from England to Ireland under a false name, committed him to prison under a false name, and brought him before a tribunal in Ireland under a statute which they knew involved a trial before an Irish jury? How would you feel yourselves as Englishmen if that man was to be submitted to trial by jury in a land inflamed against him and believing him to be a criminal, when his only crime was that he cared for England more than for Ireland?"

What the gutter-press said of this speech was tacitly condemned by the fullness with which *The Times* and the *Manchester Guardian* gave the text. On the day of its appearance Wilfrid Meynell, to whom, as to the poet Alice Meynell, the cause of the weaker nations had always been dear, received a letter from his friend in that cause, Wilfrid Scawen Blunt. To Wilfrid Meynell Casement had always been a "national hero". Blunt wrote of the speech in terms which show how profoundly he was moved:

"Dear Meynell:

"Casement's apologia is the finest document in patriotic history, finer than anything in Plutarch or elsewhere in pagan literature. . . I read it with tears this morning of anger and delight that anything so perfect in thought and word should have come from the mouth of a man of our time condemned to death. And condemned by whom?

"I should like to see the Apologia (as given in *The Times*) reprinted and distributed throughout the world. It would help to shrivel our politicians out of public life and revolutionize international law. Is there any means of communicating with the condemned? I should like to write him what I think. It is a splendid recollection for me that he spent a day with me two years ago here, and that we afterwards had a short correspondence.

"In haste to catch the post and thank you for your telegram.

"Wilfrid Scawen Blunt."

It has been said that Asquith himself, in an interview with Gertrude Bannister, suggested that Casement's life might be spared by a plea of insanity. Another letter from Wilfrid Scawen Blunt[1] to Wilfrid Meynell seems to confirm this:

"July 8, 1916.

"Dear Meynell:

"I have just heard from Miss Bannister that she has been able to convey to him in prison the substance of my letter to you and that it has pleased him. . . Though I cannot have anything to do with a plea ad misericordium on the ground of insanity, which would be too stupid! I have decided to write to Asquith as the person most responsible expressing my great admiration of Casement and my opinion of the shame he will personally incur in history if Casement is executed. . .

"Yrs. ever,

"W.S.B."

[1] Wilfrid Scawen Blunt, who had himself been in prison for his activities on behalf of Home Rule, had warm friends in the world of letters and in all the political parties. The Crabbet Club, named after his estate in Sussex where it met annually, included many famous men: George Wyndham, George Curzon, Lord Crewe, Frederick Locker, Esme Howard, Nigel Kingscote, Frank Lascelles, Mark Napier and others. Wilfrid and Alice Meynell and Hilaire Belloc were among his most constant friends.

Later Wilfrid Blunt gives us his own impression of Miss Bannister. I give it here because, from a different angle, it confirms the delineation by Professor J. H. Morgan (and indeed by all who knew her).

"Nov. 8, 1916.

"Dear Meynell:

"I hope you received the Grenfell book back. I sent it off at once though I have only got through half of it. But it does not matter as Mrs. Asquith had also just sent me her copy. I will tell you what I think of it when I have read it to the end.

"I have had an interesting visit yesterday, from Miss Bannister who is now Mrs. Sidney Parry and a near neighbour at Ewhurst. She is a charming and most interesting woman and has given me all the information I wanted about her cousin Roger. Everything she told adds to my admiration for him. He was christened a Catholic, but his mother dying when he was only 9 he was brought up by her, Miss B's, mother who was a Protestant, as she is herself, though she quite approves Sir Roger's religious ending. She says he was always 'religious minded' and always sincere and the best of men. She is a very superior woman, in mind and somewhat in looks like Charlotte Brontë, to me most attractive. . . .

"Yours very truly,
"W.S.B."

CHAPTER XII

IT HAS BEEN remarked that there was something almost macabre about the way in which sentence of death was pronounced upon Casement. It is said that the Black Cap was placed upon the head of Rufus Isaacs at a grotesque angle, while Mr. Justice Horridge, who was afflicted with a nervous twitch, appeared to be grimacing at a prisoner whose princely bearing more than confirmed his manhood. When the words "May the Lord have mercy upon your soul" were pronounced by Rufus Isaacs, a woman's voice in Court exclaimed: "And may He have mercy on yours."

In *Notable British Trials, Trial of Sir Roger Casement* (Hodge & Co., 1917), G. H. Knott, the editor, says:

"The Attorney-General has also another privilege when he appears at a trial as representing the Crown. The rule in an ordinary criminal trial as to the addresses of counsel to the jury is that the prosecuting counsel addresses the jury last if counsel for the prisoner calls witnesses or puts in evidence on the prisoner's behalf; if he does not, the last word, which is considered an advantage, lies with him. This rule, however, the Attorney-General has the right of disregarding. In any event, even when no witnesses are called by the prisoner, he claims the right to say the last word to the jury. The right has frequently been criticized as a relic of ideas about State prosecutions which no longer prevail. The Crown is really not often blood-thirsty for convictions, but the right is asserted, perhaps on the principle that one never knows what may yet turn out to be useful. Accordingly in the Casement trial, though Serjeant Sullivan did not call witnesses nor put the prisoner in the box, the Attorney-General had 'the last word.' "

The Attorney-General also had the right to allow or refuse an appeal to the House of Lords. He refused it. In his book *Famous Trials* he says that this was a question of honour and conscience with him. He says this on page 244, after calmly stating, on page 241, that Casement's diary had been found in a coat pocket, buried on the beach where Casement had landed (*v.* page 126). Delicate as his conscience may have been it could have done it no harm to have allowed another set of Judges to decide the fate of his political opponent. After his gun-running he had, with the most delicate conscience, appointed himself prosecutor; he had taken every possible advantage of the man he hated; he had refused the opportunity of an appeal, and thereby personally pronounced sentence of death upon a man more chivalrous than himself; and in his own remarkable position under Carson as an armed rebel against the Crown and Parliament of his own country, his ruthless trampling on the opponent whom he had got down was as nauseating as his talk of conscience.

In the almost unprecedented circumstances of the case, with his own armed rebellion against the Crown and British Parliament deferred by what he called a "truce" but still only in abeyance; with his own party's threat of the transfer of allegiance to Germany and his deliberately provocative taunts ringing through the mind and heart of his defeated political enemy, he dared to say "You have played and lost. I claim the forfeit of your life." His delicate conscience decided that it would not be safe to let the point of law go to the highest court in the land, or to let the responsibility for the death sentence lie on any head less conscientious than his own. He was not only the prosecuting counsel, he was the implacable enemy of that measure of Home Rule to defeat which he had been prepared to shoot his fellow-countrymen and was now determined to hang Casement.

One would have thought that in the commonest decency any man with that treason upon his conscience would at least have preferred to let the decision rest with the highest court in his own country.

After F. E. Smith had refused to allow the application for an appeal to the House of Lords, a letter from Gavan Duffy was published in *The Times* of July 28th, 1916. It states:

"Nothing more is sought from the Court of Criminal Appeal. What is wanted is that the point of law already raised, should be determined by the highest court [i.e. the House of Lords] . . . But to get the case before the House of Lords at all it is necessary that the Attorney-General and none but he—in this case not a disinterested State lawyer but the leading counsel for the prosecution—should certify that there is 'a point of law of exceptional public importance' . . . If the determination of what is high treason is not 'of exceptional public importance', the statute being worded as it is, what can be? And is it not in the public interest of this country that the point should be dealt with and settled by the highest Court in the land, and that no man, and particularly at this period of Irish history, no Irishman, should have the power to say that the determination of such a matter—one on which the life of an Irishman depends—was withheld? *Yet Sir F. E. Smith (from whom there is no appeal) whose antecedents in Ulster are well remembered, has refused the certificate and shows no inclination to reconsider his determination.*"

CHAPTER XIII

ALTHOUGH Casement at birth had been baptized in the Catholic Church, he had been brought up as a Protestant owing to the early death of his parents. His return to the Faith in which he was born was not a merely emotional conversion on the approach of death. He had written earlier:

"I don't want to jump or rush—or do anything hastily— just because time is short. It must be my deliberate act, unwavering and confirmed by all my intelligence. And alas! to-day it is not so. It is still, I find, only my heart that prompts from love, for affection for others, from associations of ideas and ideals, and not yet my full intelligence. For if it were thus the doubts could not beset me as vigorously as they do. I am not on a rock but on a bed of thorns. . . You must continue to help me as you have done in the way you wot of, and in the way you say so many more are doing."

The struggle ended, however, in an acceptance which lifted him into a new realm of certainty. He wrote:

"Give my love to all my friends, and to all who have worked for me. My last message to everyone is 'Sursum Corda', and for the rest, my goodwill to those who have taken my life, equally to all those who tried to save it. All are my brethren now."

On August 2nd, the day before he died, Casement wrote a postcard to his cousin Gertrude Bannister:

"To-morrow, St. Stephen's day,[1] I die the death I sought,

[1] Casement was quite correct in this date. August 3rd was the second festival in honour of St. Stephen. 'The Finding of St. Stephen', was instituted on the occasion of the removal of his body to a worthier burial place in 460.

155

and may God forgive the mistakes and receive the intent—
Ireland's freedom."

The last words written by Casement have been preserved
by Father McCarroll, the Prison Chaplain:

"My dominating thought was to keep Ireland out of the
war. England has no claim on us, in Law or Morality, or
Right. If I die to-morrow bury me in Ireland, and I shall
die in the Catholic Faith, for I accept it fully now. It tells
me what my heart sought long—but I saw it in the faces of
the Irish. Now I know what it was I loved in them. The
chivalry of Christ speaking through human eyes—it is from
that source all loveable things come, for Christ was the first
Knight—and now good-bye. I write still with hope—hope
that God will be with me to the end. . . ."

In the condemned cell Casement was visited every day
by Father McCarroll. Long afterwards this Chaplain wrote:

"Though thirty years have passed, the years have not
dimmed the memory of a noble—gentle, lonely soul. It was
a lonely place, the condemned cell at Pentonville Prison.
We met on the evening of the 29th of June, 1916, Feast of St.
Peter and St. Paul, and thus began a friendship which I
know has lasted far beyond the 3rd of August, 1916, the
day on which he went to God. We met on the 29th June, and
we met daily until 3rd August, until his lonely burial in the
prison yard with all the rites and ceremonies of the church.

"I was the sole mourner at his grave, yet we were not all
alone, for around were the prayers of his friends—and the
souls of noble men who thought the same thoughts and
dreamed the same dreams as Roger Casement. . . . Mass
was said in the prison chapel at 7.30 on the morning of his
execution. It was at this Mass that Roger Casement received

his first Holy Communion which was also his Viaticum. It was a day of great spiritual joy for him. He expressed a desire to go to the scaffold fasting, so that, as he said, his God might be the last food he took on earth.

"The intervening time between Mass and nine o'clock was passed in prayer. Quietly he submitted to the attentions of the executioner. With his hands bound, calmly he walked to the scaffold, repeating the words:

"'Into thy hands I commend my spirit.'

"His last words were:

"'Lord Jesus, receive my soul.'"

As the Chaplain left the prison with another priest he was approached by a newspaper man who, according to Professor Denis Gwynn, asked whether Casement, on becoming a Catholic had made a confession to him, and had he any statement to make concerning it? It is perhaps unfortunate that among those who do not understand the seal upon the lips of a priest, there might be some misinterpretation of his reply, the only reply that a priest could make at the time: "You have asked me a question which is a secret between Roger Casement and his God."

At a later date, however, Father McCarroll made a statement which, without breaking the seal upon his lips, was of a kind that no priest, however charitable, could have made about a man guilty on the moral charges. He might have said, in a more or less conventional formula, that he "made a good end", or that he had made his peace with God, but he could never have said what he actually did say. The words, of course, cannot be taken quite literally, or in the theological sense, but while the man of whom he spoke had many human failings, no one who really understands what is possible and what is impossible language at such a time, in the mouth of a Catholic Prison Chaplain of great experience, can doubt that they confirm the innocence of Roger Casement on the moral charges. The words were these:

"He was a saint. We should be praying *to* him rather than *for* him."

To those who cannot accept the words of a priest about the nature of this man, the words of Ellis, the executioner, may perhaps convey a gleam of what was utterly beyond the comprehension of his calumniators:

"The impression will ever remain on my mind of the composure of his noble countenance, the smile of contentment and happiness, as he willingly helped my assistant . . . the steady martial tread of his six feet four inches and soldierly appearance adding to the solemn echo of his prompt and coherent answers to the Roman Catholic chaplain while marching to his untimely doom. Roger Casement appeared to me the bravest man it fell to my unhappy lot to execute."[1]

[1] Quoted by M. McKeogh, *Catholic Bulletin*, August, 1928.

CHAPTER XIV

ALL THIS TIME, before the trial, during the trial and after it, the alleged diaries were being judiciously used behind the scenes to smear the character of a man who, whatever his mistakes of judgment had been, was constantly described by his friends as "the soul of honour". It was this widespread recognition of the innate chivalry of the man that inspired the movement for reprieve both in England and America. And against this movement the manipulated diaries were used with deadly effect.

Basil Thomson, in *The Scene Changes*, p. 305, says:

"Aug. 2. Bell, of the United States Embassy, told us that Mr. Page had dined with Asquith last night. Asquith told him that the Cabinet had practically decided not to interfere with Casement's sentence, and said, 'By the way, have you heard about his diary?'

" 'I have,' said Page.

" 'I should like you to see it,' said Asquith.

" 'I have,' said Page. 'What is more, I have been given photographs of some of it.'

" 'Excellent,' said Asquith, 'and you need not be particular about keeping it to yourself.' "

Shoals of telegrams, he said, were reaching him from the United States, but in all good conscience he could not interfere. The reasons he gave for this were simply the superficial and largely incorrect reasons of the cheaper newspapers. He completely ignored the political background and the deliberate and traitorous provocation which, although it might be ruled out on legalistic grounds, made all the difference in the world to the rights and wrongs of the case. The comment of the American Ambassador was brief and not flattering. Asquith could hardly have been unaware of the real background, but, as Page said: "Such is the British Prime Minister."

Twelve days before Casement's execution the real background, which had been made perfectly clear by Casement's counsel and by Casement himself at the trial, was given uncompromisingly by Bernard Shaw in a letter published in the *Manchester Guardian*, on July 22nd, 1916:

"There are several traitors in the public eye at present. At the head of them stands Christian De Wet. If De Wet is spared and Casement hanged, the unavoidable conclusion will be that Casement will be hanged, not because he is a traitor, but because he is an Irishman. We have also a group of unconvicted, and indeed unprosecuted, traitors, whose action helped very powerfully to convince Germany that she might attack France without incurring our active hostility. As all these gentlemen belong to the same political party, their impunity, if Casement be executed, will lead to the still closer conclusion that his real offence is not merely that of being an Irishman but of being a Nationalist Irishman. I see no way of getting round this."

The way of getting round it was of course the smear campaign, and the main answer to this is in the complete inability and refusal of the responsible authorities to authenticate the charges, every one of which, as has been shown, is based on false witness and defended by prevarication.

The answer is further supported by what can be proven of Casement's own character, the testimony to which is as clear and sincere as his open letter, openly published by himself, announcing his plans for the arming of the Volunteers. Through all the difficulties and complexities of his actual trial, there is not a single recorded instance of his having spoken a word that was not fearlessly true. On the other hand, the record of the other side is one long chain of trickery, evasion and falsehood, where if their acts had been honest, nothing would have been easier than to give a straightforward account.

However misguided Casement may have been in obeying his fiery impulse to meet Carson and Smith with their own weapons, there is something that sickens the heart in the spectacle of overwhelming power encompassing the death of a political enemy by calumny.

The story of the diaries has now had more than forty years to defend itself, and every request for authentication has been evaded, even when the request has been made by those upon whom official copies were deliberately imposed, and who, having been misled by them, have a clear right to an honest answer.

Character does not depend on the interpretation of a statute in Norman-French, nor can it be shattered by accusations that for their only support depend upon documents which the accusers dare not submit to expert examination. The character of Roger Casement was built up over a long period of years. The indirect evidence for it is as strong as the testimony of those who knew him most intimately. It appears in the testimony of men as different as Joseph Conrad, Stephen Gwynn, E. D. Morel, the prison chaplain and the man at whose hands he died. It appears in the testimony of his devoted women friends Mrs. John Richard Green,

Sylvia Lynd and his relative Mrs. Sidney Parry, whose unremitting efforts to save Casement are described by Professor J. H. Morgan as a most moving instance of belief in a grievously wronged man.

Moreover, and this is of the utmost importance, the *kind* of testimony they give has never in the history of the world been given to a man of bad moral character. Men addicted to vice have often had their champions on other grounds; but this championship has never in history been expressed in the *kind* of language used about this man, not only from the pulpit of Westminster Abbey, but from the hearts and minds of upright men and women who were his personal friends. It is not the language of that ambiguous tolerance indifferent to all moral considerations. It is the sincere language of men and women profoundly aware of those moral considerations and profoundly indignant at the charges brought against a man whose mind was like an open book to them.

An instance, and it is only one of scores, is a letter from Mr. Seamus MacCall, the Irish historian:

"Against all the efforts of his detractors I can set the fact that every one of Roger's relatives I ever met, and every honest man among my acquaintances who knew him, had the greatest possible admiration for his idealism, his humanitarianism, his generosity, his morals and his personal character."

Robert Lynd, one of the most distinguished essayists of his day, wrote to *The Nation* of May 13th, 1916, his own protest against the smear campaign; and again it was couched in the *kind* of language which has never been used, even by the most tolerant, of a degenerate such as that depicted by Sir Ernley Blackwell and Sir Basil Thomson.

"As the case of Sir Roger Casement is at present *sub judice*, I do not propose to discuss the question of his guilt or innocence in regard to the accusations made against him. But I must protest when one of the least self-seeking and most open-handed of men—a man who has lived not for his career but for the liberation of those who are oppressed and poor and enslaved—is dismissed with all the *clichés* of contempt. . . Even those who, like myself, have been diametrically opposed to his recent policy, can never lose our admiration and affection for everything in him that was noble and compassionate."

CHAPTER XV

CASEMENT himself, according to three of his lawyers, knew nothing of the moral charges brought against him until he was in the condemned cell. Michael Francis Doyle, the American Attorney who had been retained in Casement's defence, has testified that when Casement was told about the diaries:

"He was astounded at first and then he became bitterly indignant. He said many angry things about England's methods of fighting Irishmen, and spoke of the conspiracy in the British Legation at Christiania to have him 'knocked on the head'. He referred to the reputed habits of certain Englishmen among his persecutors. But still he said that he could not get it into his mind that the British would stoop to such a forgery to destroy his character. . . *It was clear to Gavan Duffy and me that diary was not his*; and he emphatically repudiated it."

Casement instructed his solicitor to write to the Home Secretary asking if the charges might be submitted to him so that they might be answered. To this letter from Mr. Gavan Duffy, the solicitor responsible for the defence, the Home Secretary, the present Lord Samuel, gave no reply, not even an acknowledgment. Perhaps he too, like subsequent Home Secretaries, was unable to vouch for the existence or non-existence of the documents in question.

In my first chapter I dealt with one aspect of the statement attributed to and subsequently denied by Serjeant Sullivan, that Casement had confessed his guilt to him on the moral charges. Other aspects of this statement must now be considered.

One of these, incompatible with the clear evidence of the two lawyers quoted above, appears in a letter of Serjeant Sullivan. The Serjeant, in his old age, was a little piqued because, as he says in his interview in November, 1954, with Mr. René MacColl, none of Casement's other biographers had seen fit to seek him out for source material. He had apparently completely forgotten that one of the most recent biographers, Dr. Herbert O. Mackey, F.R.C.S., had interviewed him at some length only five months before. However, when the venerable Serjeant was approached as a preliminary to an interview by Mr. René MacColl, the competent correspondent of the *Daily Express*, he naturally pricked up his ears and dropped a bomb with chain reactions. In a letter to Mr. MacColl he says:

"It was in Court that Travers Humphreys handed me the envelope, stating that Freddie ordered him to put it in my hands. *I refused to read it as I knew all about it from Casement himself*. He would not accept my assurance that the Crown could not use it, and instructed me to explain to the Jury that the filthy practices and the rhapsodical glorification of them were inseparable from genius, and I was to cite a list of all truly great men to prove it."

Here, at least, was one statement on which Serjeant Sullivan could be pinned down, and he was quite firmly pinned down by the statements of the two other lawyers quoted above. Shortly afterwards, therefore, Serjeant Sullivan wrote a letter to the *Irish Times* in which he said:

"On reflection, I perceive that he (Casement) neither affirmed nor denied authenticity. He took up the attitude

165

that we pigmies could not understand the conduct of great men and had no right to pass judgment on it. He was neither glorifying nor repudiating what was alleged against him."

Further, Serjeant Sullivan himself, in another letter to the *Irish Times*, has now repudiated the interpretation placed upon the interview with Mr. MacColl, and he evidently wishes to do this without impugning the competence of his interviewer. In this letter he eats most of his words and allows the rest to melt in his mouth:

"Some misapprehension may arise from Mr. MacColl's letter in to-day's issue (April 25th). He very properly quotes from a communication of mine what Casement said to me about the characteristics of genius. When the public were informed of the existence and nature of these documents, Casement was very anxious that I should enlighten the multitude on this peculiar feature of genius, which he said was invariable in all great men through the ages. He left it to me to supply the names and details, but he was extremely anxious that this mission should be carried out whenever the fact of the diaries was revealed.

"*He told me nothing about the diaries or about himself* but Mr. MacColl may well translate this peculiar communication as being a boastful confession in view of the fact that no refutation of the authorship of the diaries appeared in Casement's lifetime, when it might have helped to save him."

In each of Serjeant Sullivan's letters he flatly contradicts a statement which he made in an earlier letter or in the interview with Mr. MacColl, e.g. in one passage he said that Casement glorified the vice charged, that it was "inseparable from genius". In another letter he says that Casement neither glorified the moral offence nor repudiated it. In another passage he speaks contemptuously of the perfectly clear-cut statements of Mr. Michael Doyle and Mr. Gavan Duffy. Then, denying that the former had seen Casement at all, at the same time he admits that the interview took place in order that he may give the wrong explanation of the indignation which Casement showed at that interview, saying that he was indignant at the methods used and not at the charge. In a recent letter to me Mr. Doyle says: "I visited him each day during his trial. . . He frankly denied to me that he ever wrote such a diary. I believed him—and still do."

Memory, perhaps? The only charitable explanation is that after nearly half a century the Serjeant's memory has become a little confused. As we have seen, he was unwell at the time of the trial. He says that he was utterly exhausted mentally and physically. His actual words, in a letter to Mr. MacColl, are:

"Three days and nights of worrying caused me to break down and fall senseless while addressing the Jury. I had used up every red corpuscle in my body."

Shortly before his breakdown, some of the statements made to the Court were all too symptomatic of a mind confused by sheer exhaustion.

In such condition it is more than probable that some misunderstanding arose over what Casement said in one of those long streams of talk described by Gerald Campbell at an earlier date. There exists, for instance, that statement about the great men (Mazzini, Garibaldi, Washington and others) whom Casement too rashly took as exemplars for his own "treason". There exists in his own hand a letter written from Brixton Prison, in which he asks a friend to collect information on such names for him. It seems hardly likely, unless he was indeed insane (which was denied by both prosecution and defence) that he wished to compile two such lists, one heroic and the other vicious, for submission to the Jury.

Serjeant Sullivan's own opinion on the authenticity of the diaries, at a distance of forty years, with a memory so obviously confused, is hardly acceptable. He had refused even to look at the typed copy. In the letter of April 25th, as we have seen, he said that Casement told him "nothing about the diaries or about himself". This is again not reconcilable with his other statement that in the event of the diary being brought to light by the British Government Casement wished him to tell the Jury that the offences mentioned were characteristic of all great men. How could they possibly discuss such an elaborate and insane procedure if the subject had not been mentioned by either of them?

If this conversation between client and leading counsel unattended by the solicitor, in itself an unusual proceeding, ever took place (and the solicitor affirmed that the dates made it impossible), the conversation, without reference to the diary or to Casement himself must have been on very vague and general lines. It is just conceivable that Casement, who had written of the "terrible disease" with which Sir Hector MacDonald had been afflicted, may have caught up some remark with which Serjeant Sullivan tried to introduce the subject, and launched into one of his characteristic tirades against what he regarded as the wrong treatment of that "terrible disease" which he looked on as a subject for the doctor rather than for criminal law. He may even have told the exhausted Serjeant Sullivan that Julius Caesar and other irrelevant characters were afflicted with it; and at the end of half an hour Serjeant Sullivan, with "not a corpuscle of red blood left" and a mind too tired even to listen to irrelevancies, may have misunderstood the gist of the argument. This was even more probable after forty years.

On the other hand, we have the perfectly clear statements of the other distinguished Counsel, Mr. Michael Francis Doyle, the American attorney, who, as he says (letter of December 12th, 1956), "talked with Casement more than any of his legal staff".

Mr. Doyle's statement (p. 164) strikes one as an extraordinarily accurate characterization of Casement himself, his living and speaking likeness as it appeared to his friends. We see him here with his extraordinary flow of speech, blurting out quite frankly everything that came into his mind, at one moment angry, and at another—with a certain magnanimity—unable to believe in the baseness that had angered him. I cannot doubt that this is the true picture, not only of the man but of the exact way in which he received his first information about the diaries. But if this be so, it makes utter nonsense of the inconsistent picture given by Serjeant Sullivan. It seems quite impossible that, as a part of his defence, Casement should have suggested to him the insane glorification of a "terrible disease", as he calls it (a glorification which Serjeant Sullivan himself "on reflection" affirms never took place), or of that evil which he so condemned in his Munich diary. It is equally impossible that, having suggested this defence to one of his counsel, he should have convinced his other two lawyers very shortly afterwards that he was completely taken by surprise and that the diary was not his. He never saw the typescript.

Mr. MacColl in 1954 says Serjeant Sullivan at the age of ninety-three is as alert and spry as ever. *Who's Who* has stated for a good many years that the Serjeant was born in 1871. If Mr. MacColl is right, Serjeant Sullivan somehow or other has forgotten ten years of his life. But if, as one hopes, Mr. MacColl is wrong, one cannot help wondering why he assigns such antiquity to an interlocutor so fruitful of surprises and with so interesting a conversational gift.

But there are flaws more serious than this. I will not enter here into the propriety of a statement by counsel which has already been criticized with considerable heat by eminent members of his own profession as contrary to their high tradition of the relationship between counsel and client. But there is one extraordinary feature of it to which a layman may fairly call attention.

"Freddie" Smith offered the alleged diary to the defence, said Serjeant Sullivan, and adds:

"*His Majesty's Government were unsure about executing Casement. They were clutching at straws to save him. They were angling for America and they knew that the execution would be seized on for glorifying him in America. F. E. Smith was searching desperately for an excuse to thwart the public of their victim.*"

Examine those sentences carefully. Freddie Smith, who subsequently threatened the Government with his resignation as Attorney-General if Casement were not hanged, and who boasted of his delight at the hanging, offered the alleged diary to the defence in order that they might plead insanity and so "thwart the public"—which was at that moment being inflamed against Casement by the judicious use of that very diary.

What was F. E. Smith's motive? It was certainly not to save Casement, whom he hated as a political enemy. It was irredeemably to smear his enemy, and perhaps more particularly the cause (Home Rule) with which his victim had been associated, by inducing the defence to accept, as its basis, the truth of the moral charges against one of its leaders. He knew perfectly well that the judges were likely to regard the evidence of insanity as insufficient even with what Serjeant Sullivan calls "the *honest* co-operation of the prosecution"—who did not believe their victim to be insane. Therefore Casement would be both smeared *and* hanged.

Failing this, if the judges, also with "honest" co-operation, accepted a plea in which they did not believe, Casement would be lodged in a lunatic asylum, an end that would serve almost equally well. The prosecution could not bring these diaries into Court on a charge of treason. Ah, but if the defence would only co-operate! And if the diaries could not be brought into Court by the prosecution there remained the by-play about the sheet of paper, transformed into a diary during the trial, which might, by . . . judicious means, convey to the Jury and to the outside world a good deal of what could not be spoken.

Was F. E. Smith blissfully unconscious when in his book *Famous Trials* he affirms, without blinking an eyelid, that Casement's diary was found in his overcoat pocket on the beach at Tralee?

In his interview with René MacColl Serjeant Sullivan makes an admission as extraordinary in its legal aspect as in what, in a less tragic case, might be called its lack of humour. If Casement were adjudged insane, he said, it might have saved his life. Yes, but—with every appearance of noble satisfaction—"I did not give Casement any option in the matter. . . . It would only have dirtied him. . . . *Better death than dishonour.*"

Then, his client having been successfully hanged, Serjeant Sullivan, in confused old age, calmly bestows the dishonour upon him, and excuses himself by saying that Casement has no relative living, which again is untrue.

At the very time when Serjeant Sullivan gave Casement "no option", the Serjeant was well aware of the smear campaign that was being conducted behind the scenes. He condemns the dissemination of the diaries by saying that "the British Government of the day wasn't very particular about what they were prepared to do to damp down the pro-Irish and anti-British sentiment in America. I believe it [the smear campaign] was done at some time or other before the U.S.A. entered the war. What people do in war is unpredictable. Perfectly decent men will do perfectly shocking things in the prevailing hysteria."

On Serjeant Sullivan's own testimony Gavan Duffy told him that the diaries had been shown before the trial to American correspondents in London, yet he refuses to inspect them, look at them, or "have anything to do with them", even to inquire about their authenticity, and he gives his client "no option", makes no effort to protect his client against the moral charges, merely dismissing them as irrelevant to the charge of treason. Irrelevant as they were, they went far to prevent a reprieve. The helpless defendant had indeed no option but death *and* dishonour.

When the American lawyer Mr. Doyle learned of the use that was being made of the diaries, he told the solicitor, Mr. Gavan Duffy, that Casement should be informed. There followed the interview described on a previous page, in which Casement indignantly repudiated the charges. Mr. Doyle continues:

"When he calmed down he asked us if we had seen the 'diary' and if we knew what form it was in, whether in the nature of a book or separated sheets, or otherwise. He also requested us to obtain quotations of it.

"Gavan Duffy and myself then tried to locate this 'diary'. We had learned that the Police had obtained possession of some personal effects Casement had left behind in London. Gavan Duffy called upon the Attorney-General's Office and requested to see any personal effects of Casement in the custody of the British, especially the alleged diary. He was referred to the Home Office. Both Gavan Duffy and myself then called at the Home Office and made request to be allowed to see Casement's personal effects, and particularly the 'diary'. We were referred to Scotland Yard. At Scotland Yard we repeated our request, again stressing our wish to see the diary. We were referred back again to the Home Office. We visited the Attorney-General's office the second time and were advised that the personal effects and papers of Casement were not under its charge.

"On our next visit to Casement we told him of our inability to obtain information about the 'diary'. He stated he thought they might be using some notes from his records concerning official investigations he had conducted, but that there could be nothing referring to any personal acts of perversion, except what was false and malicious. He urged us to use every means to get all the information we could so he could answer the insinuations.

"I never saw the alleged diary or any part thereof, or even any statement therefrom, in any photostatic or other form, nor did I meet anyone who said he actually saw the diary or even a photostatic copy of it.

"As the efforts of Gavan Duffy and myself to see the alleged diary, or to get evidence of it, continued without success, Casement (through Gavan Duffy on his behalf) wrote a letter from his prison to the Secretary for Home Affairs asking permission to answer these false and malicious insinuations, and for information as to the contents of this 'diary'. This letter was never answered. We later inquired from the secretary of Mr. Herbert Samuel, who was the Secretary for Home Affairs, and Mr. Samuel's secretary denied ever having received such a letter. Up to the time he died, Roger Casement never saw this 'diary' or any part of its alleged contents."

Let the reader consider this: The typed copy of the diary was offered to the defence only at the earlier date when the prosecution was "honestly" offering to co-operate with the defence if they would accept the diary as true and plead insanity. Serjeant Sullivan refused to look at it in that connection; but at the precise moment when authentication was first demanded by Casement's lawyers inspection was refused. It has been refused ever since and for no conceivable reason but one: that the original documents will not stand up to it.

Let the reader also remember that while this authentication was refused to the legal representatives of a man on trial for his life, typed copies and photostatic extracts were being shown to selected persons both in England and America, *through official channels.* On the eve of Casement's execution, as we have seen, Asquith, the Prime Minister, told Walter Hines Page, the American Ambassador, that he "need not be particular" about keeping the contents of the diaries to himself.

That very moment when authentication was first demanded by the defence was the beginning of the long and disgraceful series of evasions, prevarications, self-contradictory statements and plain lies which have met every request for authentication for nearly half a century.

From letters in the National Library of Ireland it is clear that Gavan Duffy replied to several correspondents, who wanted him to do something to check the organized campaign of calumny (which approached its crescendo some weeks after the trial), that no legal step could be taken unless the Government Department responsible was identified, and this he had failed to do. Two days after Casement's execution Professor J. H. Morgan,[1] Serjeant Sullivan's legal adviser and by far the most eminent of the lawyers in the case, wrote to F. E. Smith a letter of which he sent a copy in his own handwriting to Gavan Duffy. This is now in the National Library of Ireland. It begins:

"Dear Mr. Attorney,

"You will remember that at my interview with you on July 14th you expressed some concern lest 'questions should be raised' as to the use of a certain diary attributed to Roger

---

[1] Professor J. H. Morgan served in the war as Brigadier-General and was mentioned in despatches, so may be absolved of any sympathy with treason. In the Casement trial he was legal adviser to Serjeant Sullivan merely on the constitutional aspect of the treason charges. He was afterwards Honorary Adviser to the U.S. War Crimes Commission at Nuremberg.

Casement, and that at the subsequent interview of Mr. Jones and myself with you on July 19th you—in reply to a representation made by Mr. Jones as to complaints on the part of Casement's friends that attempts had been made to prejudice members of the public against him by revealing the contents of the said diary—*assured us that there was 'not a word of truth in these complaints'.*"

Professor Morgan then referred to *The Times* protest of August 4th as a direct contradiction of what F. E. Smith had said.

The letter of Professor Morgan thus establishes that on July 14th, three days before Casement's appeal was heard and when such papers as the *Weekly Despatch* and the *News of the World* were commenting openly on "Casement's diaries", F. E. Smith expressed his concern to Professor Morgan lest questions should be raised as to the use of the alleged diary, and when Morgan next interviewed Smith, a day or two after Casement's appeal had been rejected, Jones was with him. And in answer to Jones' protest, F. E. Smith calmly denied that there was any truth in complaints that the diary had been used to prejudice public opinion against Casement!

This denial may be illuminated by a letter now in the Casement Collection in the National Library of Ireland, from Mr. Bulmer Hobson to Senator McHugh, dated November 2nd, 1956.

"My statement about Smith at the trial [his use of the diary behind the scenes] is based on the following facts. About the year 1922 I met the late Sir James O'Connor at the house of a friend. O'Connor was Attorney-General in

Ireland in 1916 and later Lord Justice of Appeal. He was retired when the Free State was established. O'Connor told me that he was in London on business at the time of the Casement trial and, wanting to see a celebrated state trial, he attended all the sittings of the Court. At the end of the first day, after he had left the Court, F. E. Smith (whom he hardly knew) came running down the corridor after him, calling out, 'Here, O'Connor, I want to show you something.' He then handed O'Connor a photostat of a page of the indecent diary. O'Connor looked at it and handed it back.

"O'Connor had no political sympathy with Casement but he was shocked and disgusted at the impropriety of the Attorney-General of England peddling dirty stories in this way about a man he was prosecuting on a charge of treason."

Morgan's letter to Duffy indicates that he had intended writing to *The Times* but had decided to protest to Smith instead. Duffy's reply said that there was no remedy, except "to horsewhip F. E. Smith". He might have used even stronger language if he had known of Sir Ernley Blackwell's Memorandum to the Cabinet on the judicious use of the diary—the Cabinet before which Sir F. E. Smith had laid it, and of which he was a member.

Casement's appeal was heard on July 17th: once it had been rejected, Smith knew that nothing stood between Casement and death but his *fiat*, which he so conscientiously refused.

No Government ever lost dignity or prestige by honestly facing facts and making amends to a wronged man. The Government of the day lost nothing when Gladstone made his famous speech in the House of Commons on the Pigott forgeries.

"I ask you individually, man by man," he said, "to place

yourselves in the position of the honourable member (Charles Stewart Parnell) as the victim of this frightful outrage. Is it possible in doing this, after all his cares, all his suffering, all he has gone through, and I believe there is no parallel to it for at least two hundred years, that you can fail to feel that something remains due to him? No, then give such a JUDGMENT as will bear the scrutiny of the heart and of the conscience of every man, when he betakes himself to his chamber and is still. . . Accede, to our demand, accede to our prayer, and grant this late, this miserable, this perhaps scanty reparation of an enormous, unheard-of wrong."

The *Annual Register* for 1900 states:

"Mr. Gladstone held the house in silence until the close, when from all sides applause broke forth unstinted and unrestrained by party feeling."

If Roger Casement had died only a few years earlier he would probably have had his memorial in Westminster Abbey, near those of Livingstone and Stanley. He was buried near Crippen in the yard of Pentonville Prison. Among the last words he wrote were:

"Do not let me lie in this dreadful place."

On the morning after the sentence of death for treason had been executed, Professor Morgan wrote a letter to the Home Secretary, Mr. Samuel, making a most moving appeal that the request of Casement's relatives, friends and countrymen should be granted, and that his body should be allowed to rest in his native Antrim. The letter reads:

"Dear Mr. Samuel:

"The day before yesterday I called at the House of Commons to see you in order to support the request of Miss

Gertrude Bannister that the body of Roger Casement might be handed over to her for private burial. I did this because I was deeply moved by the distress of a noble woman whose unflinching devotion to her cousin through the long-drawn agony of his trial was such as to provoke my profound admiration and regret. I did not—indeed as counsel I could not—support the movement for reprieve. But he has paid the full penalty—he has not only died a felon's death on the scaffold, but before dying he was publicly degraded of all his honours, a step for which I believe there is no precedent in any treason case in the last 300 years. The law has therefore exacted its uttermost.

"Under these circumstances it is surely not asking too much to ask that the pitiful request of his relatives be granted. Roger Casement is now beyond the reach of human vengeance; it cannot matter to him whether his body remains in a felon's grave in Pentonville or not. But it matters a great deal to this unhappy lady, sorrowing under a sorrow almost too grievous for any man or woman to bear. I cannot conceive any petition which it would be easier for the authorities to grant and harder for any humane person to refuse. It is not for me to urge any question of policy, though I can imagine few things more likely to exasperate Irish opinion than an implacable severity which wounds the living while it is powerless to harm the dead. Moreover *there is a very strong opinion abroad—* The Times *gives expression to it this morning—that someone in authority 'inspired' a campaign of malignant and studied calumny against the prisoner which was not only not necessary to the course of justice, but calculated to pervert it.* It is surely highly undesirable that any impression of ruthlessness should get abroad?

"But be that as it may, I do beg of you on grounds of

179

humanity to reconsider your decision. Miss Bannister is, I understand, prepared to give every guarantee as to privacy."

It is surely time that England acceded to the repeated requests of the Irish Government that the body of Roger Casement be allowed to rest in his native country, and that the Home Office should review the whole case—the magnificent work for humanity accomplished by Sir Roger Casement almost single-handed and honoured all over the world; the strain of the appalling things he had witnessed; the consequent emotional disturbance which led him as an Irishman into thinking that armed rebellion of Englishmen against their own Government in the North would justify similar action, not against but in favour of his own country, where thousands feel these things passionately and will never forget them while his empty grave in Antrim awaits him.

Surely in the name of common honesty it is possible to sweep away a miserable network of evasions, contradictions and palpable lies, and meet honest questions with honest answers. Surely it is possible to repudiate a grievous wrong committed in the heat of war nearly half a century ago, and accede to what Lord Attlee called the reasonable request of the Irish Government that the body of this wronged man should be returned to his native country. This request has been repeatedly made to the British Government and stubbornly refused by a stupid and bull-headed bureaucracy for no conceivable reason, except for that one damnable purpose of the smear campaign, which, even if the forgeries had been genuine, is now universally admitted to have been infamous.

The granting of the Irish Government's request would have its reward in history.

APPENDICES

APPENDIX I

DURING THE sittings, on May 18th-19th, 1916, of the Royal Commission on the Rebellion in Ireland, important facts were established, though the general public in England had completely lost sight of them during the trial of Sir Roger Casement. The Right Hon. Augustine Birrell, K.C., questioned by the Chairman, the Right Hon. Lord Hardinge of Penshurst, K.G., P.C., etc., on disaffection in Ireland, said:

"There were a number of contributory causes which lately have created the utmost excitement. . . First, growing doubts about the actual advent of Home Rule. If the Home Rule Bill had *not* been placed on the Statute Book there *must* have been both in Ireland and the United States a great and dangerous explosion of rage and disappointment which when the war broke out would have assumed the most alarming proportions. In Ireland all (outside parts of Ulster) would have joined hands, whilst our reports from Washington tell us what the effect on America would have been. Still, even with Home Rule on the Statute Book the chance of its ever becoming a *fact* was so uncertain, the outstanding difficulty about Ulster was so obvious, and the details of the measure itself were so unattractive, and difficult to transmute into telling platform phrases, that *Home Rule* as an emotional flag fell out of daily use in current Irish life. Second: But in Ireland whenever constitutional and Parliamentary procedure cease to be of absorbing influence . . . other methods . . . come rapidly to the surface. Third: The Ulster Rebellion,

183

gun-running at Larne, the Covenant, the Provisional Government and its members, its plan of warfare in Belfast, its armed Volunteers and public drillings, and all the rest of the 'pomp and circumstance' of revolution, had the most prodigious effect upon disloyalists *elsewhere*. Fourth: Then came the war on the 4th of August, 1914. . . Fifth: The Coalition Government *with* Sir Edward Carson in it! It is impossible to describe or overestimate the effect of this in Ireland. . . This step seemed to make an end of Home Rule and strengthened the Sinn Feiners enormously all over the country. . . . The war upset all our calculations. . . ."

The Right Hon. Sir James Dougherty, K.C.B., K.C.V.O., Under-Secretary for Ireland from July, 1908, to October, 1914, made a statement before the Commission:

". . . I do not propose to deal at any length with . . . the gun-running at Larne and Howth. It is at this moment probably inadvisable to say much on those subjects; but I may be permitted to observe that to arrive at a fair judgment and to apportion responsibility it is necessary to bear in mind the sequence of events. The National Volunteers were the response of Nationalist Ireland to the Volunteer movement in Unionist Ulster; and the gun-running at Howth was but the natural sequel to the gun-running at Larne."

APPENDIX II

I HAVE REFRAINED in the text of this book from mention-
ing the extraordinary story told by Mr. Singleton-Gates in a
letter to *The Times* and, with some serious differences, in an
article in *The Spectator*.

In his letter to *The Times* Mr. Singleton-Gates says that
he had "continuous access" to the officially typed copy of the
diary between 1922 and 1925, and "*sight*" of the originals
which, he says, enabled him to confirm certain entries in the
typed copy. This, by itself (as was clearly shown before on
page 113), proves nothing so far as interpolations and
additions are concerned. Moreover, when pressed to say
exactly what he meant by "sight" of the original as distinct
from "continuous access" to a typed copy and whether he
was allowed leisure to examine the original thoroughly, his
reply, if not evasive, was completely unsatisfactory as to a
method of authentication. Apparently he did not compare
the typed copy with the original, but merely took some notes
which he had made of certain entries in the typed copy, and
found that they corresponded with certain entries in what
were alleged to be the original documents. For some reason
he conceals the name of "a person in high authority indeed"
who had allowed him sight of the documents, at a time when,
as the Home Secretary in 1926 (Mr. Clynes) publicly
stated, it had "*long* been the settled policy" of his Department to allow no such privilege to anyone. And why
to Mr. Singleton-Gates when it was denied to historians and
experts? The "continuous access" between 1922 and 1925,

185

moreover, is open to various interpretations. Most people, reading Mr. Singleton-Gates' letter, would suppose the accent to be a privilege which had been accorded to him and which had been expressly denied by the Home Secretary to anyone else; as if, for instance, a mysterious door had been opened to him in some Government Department. But in his article in *The Spectator* on June 15th, 1956, he gives exactly the opposite impression. Here we are told, in the best cloak and dagger style, that a mysterious person in authority, whose name cannot be mentioned, knocked at *his* door and delivered to him a package containing officially typed "copies of diaries" attributed to Roger Casement. This person in authority had been *asked* to come to him (why?) by a person of even higher authority whose name, according to Mr. Singleton-Gates, must forever remain unknown.

The answer to the "why" in the sentence above is that this whole business is simply a prolongation of the original wrong. I am assured by the Unionist Member for Belfast that he has recently been shown Mr. Singleton-Gates' copy, which the latter has also shown to Mr. Frank MacDermott and to Mr. MacColl. The latest suggestion, as this book goes to press, is that a *microfilm copy* of this *typed copy* of the elusive originals will soon be made available to serious historians.

All this ridiculous mystery and multiplication of copies of copies of phantom originals only emphasizes the need for a proper and straightforward inquiry by qualified experts.

APPENDIX III

IN VIEW OF THE fact that evidence from Germany was being produced by the prosecution, the following communication from Michael Francis Doyle, who is still in practice in America, sent to me on January 3rd, 1957, will illustrate the obstacles that were placed in the way of the defence:

"One of the reasons for my appearing in this case was to go to Germany and obtain evidence on Casement's behalf. When this fact was presented to the Attorney-General's office, Mr. Duffy was flatly told I would not be permitted to return to England, if I went to Germany for evidence. The matter was much discussed among counsel at the time. It was thought that my services would be of special value because I had been in Germany for a brief period previously at the American Embassy under Mr. Gerard, working out plans for the assistance of our countrymen caught in the turmoil of the early days of the war.[1] I spoke German, was familiar with German affairs, and had covered many parts of Germany in assisting Americans to whose aid I was sent by President Wilson direct, with a fund at my disposal for their assistance. . . ."

In the same letter, Mr. Doyle, to whom I had communicated my general findings in this book, remarks:

"There is no doubt in my mind that your judgment is correct. This plot of the diaries was the villainous scheme of Frederick E. Smith. He had a particular special and personal

[1]The United States did not enter the war until 1917.

interest in trying to destroy Casement's moral character. . . .
Smith was bitter, knowing that his actions were already compared with Casement's, and, not satisfied with his judicial
destruction, he was determined to put him outside the circle
of human relationship when he developed the moral charges
against him."

LIST OF NAMES

Massingham, H. W., 10
Mazzini, 38
Meynell, Alice, 149, 150n.
Meynell, Wilfrid, 149-50
Mitchel, John, 38
Montague, Ewan, 103
Monteith, Robert, 91-2
Morel, E. D., 45, 60, 161
Morgan, Prof. J. H., 100, 122, 162, 175-8
Moriarty, Attorney-General, 186

Napier, Mark, 150n.
Nation, The, 162
Nevinson, H. W., 140
New Statesman, 12
Newman, Mrs. Nina, 92n.
News of the World, 176
Nicholson, Arthur, 77
Nicoll, Sir William Robertson, 10
Normand, Armando, 16, 49-51, 54, 102, 105-6, 108-9, 111, 115
Norwich, Lord, 103
Noyes, Alfred, 23

O'Connor, Sir James, 176-7
O'Hegarty, P. S., 105
Oliver, Sir Sydney, 10

Page, Walter Hines, 12, 19, 159-60, 175
Parnell, Charles Stewart, 44, 178
Parry, Mrs. Sidney. See Bannister, Gertrude
Peruvian Amazon Rubber Company, 47, 58
Phillips, Rev. Thomas, 10
Putumayo, 47-59, 60-4

Quinn, John, 101, 106
Quinn, Patrick, 99-100

Raleigh, Sir Walter, 79
Redmond, John, 19, 35, 78
Royal Commission on the Rebellion in Ireland, 33, 37, 183
Ryan, Father F. M., 129

Samuel, Herbert (Lord), 164, 174, 178
Sanchez, Ramon, 49
Sandford, General Henry, 39
Scott, C. P., 10
Sealey, Stanley, 54
Shaw, Bernard, 160
Shorter, Clement, 10
Singleton-Gates, Mr., 15-16, 185-6
Smith, Sir F. E. (Lord Birkenhead), 16, 28, 36, 38, 59, 65, 72, 77, 93, 101, 104, 107-8, 119-27, 129, 135, 138-9, 152-4, 161, 170-1, 175-7, 187-8
Spectator, The, 185-6
Spring-Rice, Sir Cecil, 11, 95, 101
Sullivan, Serjeant, 16, 30, 129-39, 153, 164-72, 174-5
Swinburne, A. C., 39

Taft, President, 62
Thomson, Sir Basil, 14-17, 19-20, 63, 88, 93, 96-104, 106-7, 109-10, 119, 128, 159, 162
Tillett, Ben, 10
Times, The, 9, 26, 30, 63, 96, 149, 154, 176-7, 179, 185-6

Ulster Volunteers, 33, 35-7, 67, 70, 72, 143-4, 186

Vasquez, Filomene, 51, 53
Voltaire, 121

Webb, Sidney and Beatrice, 10
Weekly Despatch, 176
Wells, H. G., 122
Wilson, Woodrow, 12, 19, 187
Winchester, Bishop of, 10
Wyndham, George, 150n.

Yates, V., 13
Yeats, W. B., 11-12, 20
Younger, Mr., 23

Zangwill, Israel, 10
Zerkusen, Franz H. J., 91
Zola, 121